SPORTS HEROES AND LEGENDS™

Sandy Koufax

Read all of the books in this exciting,
action-packed biography series!

Hank Aaron

Muhammad Ali

Lance Armstrong

Barry Bonds

Joe DiMaggio

Tim Duncan

Dale Earnhardt Jr.

Lou Gehrig

Derek Jeter

Sandy Koufax

Michelle Kwan

Mickey Mantle

Jesse Owens

Alex Rodriguez

Wilma Rudolph

Ichiro Suzuki

Tiger Woods

SPORTS HEROES AND LEGENDS™

Sandy Koufax

by Matt Doeden

 Twenty-First Century Books/Minneapolis

For my grandparents, Gordon and Verda

Twenty-First Century Books
A division of Lerner Publishing Group
241 First Avenue North
Minneapolis, MN 55401 U.S.A.

Website address: www.lernerbooks.com

Cover photograph:
© Focus on Sport/Getty Images

Library of Congress Cataloging-in-Publication Data

Doeden, Matt.
    Sandy Koufax / by Matt Doeden.
       p.   cm. — (Sports heroes and legends)
    Includes bibliographical references and index.
    ISBN-13: 978-0-8225-5961-0 (lib. bdg. : alk. paper)
    ISBN-10: 0-8225-5961-7 (lib. bdg. : alk. paper)
    1. Koufax, Sandy, 1935– —Juvenile literature. 2. Baseball players—United States—Biography—Juvenile literature. I. Title. II. Series.
GV865.K67D64 2007
796.357092—dc22   2006005882

Manufactured in the United States of America
1 2 3 4 5 6 – JR – 12 11 10 09 08 07

Contents

World Series Hero

Sport has no grander stage than game seven of a World Series. It's the final game of a grueling season, with everything on the line and almost no margin for error—the game every kid and every ballplayer dreams about.

When Los Angeles Dodgers pitcher Sandy Koufax walked to the mound for game seven of the 1965 World Series against the Minnesota Twins, all of his team's hopes rested on his left arm. The twenty-nine-year-old lefty was the best pitcher in the big leagues. He was pitching on only two days of rest (unheard of in modern baseball), and he was making his third start in just eight days. Even more amazing, he was pitching despite a painful condition called arthritis in his left elbow. Baseball fans knew that Sandy could shut down any lineup—even the powerful Twins—but could he do it on so little rest? Did his arm have the strength?

As the game got under way, the Metropolitan Stadium crowd of 50,596 seemed unusually quiet. Twins manager Sam Mele later said, "I think everybody could sense . . . that it's Koufax out there. You can't get too excited because this guy's going to knock the jubilance out of you, you know?"

Still, the Twins had won all three games played at the Met, in Bloomington, Minnesota, while the Dodgers had won the three games played in Los Angeles, California. It was up to Sandy to break the tie. The opposing starter was Jim Kaat, another tough lefty. Kaat, whose 1965 record had been 18–11, had beaten Sandy in game two but lost to him in game five. This day, he knew he'd have to be perfect.

"If I give up a run, the game is over," Kaat told a teammate before the game.

Kaat did his job in the top of the first, so Sandy entered a 0–0 game that had the look and feel of a classic pitchers' duel. His first batter was Zoilo Versalles, the American League's Most Valuable Player (MVP). Sandy struck him out on six pitches. Sandy got the next batter, Joe Nossek, to ground out. But he went on to walk the next two batters, causing many to wonder if Dodger manager Walter Alston had made a wise choice in starting Sandy over the more rested Don Drysdale. After the second walk, Drysdale began warming up in the Dodger bullpen, getting ready to replace the struggling lefty.

But Sandy had other plans. He quickly worked the count against catcher Earl Battey to 1–2 (1 ball and 2 strikes), then struck him out with a big, diving curveball. The inning—and the Twins' scoring threat—was over.

Kaat and Sandy dueled through three shutout innings. Then in the top of the fourth, the Dodgers got on the scoreboard when Lou Johnson hit a shot down the left-field line. The ball bounced off the foul pole for a home run. The Dodgers added another run in the inning, giving Sandy a 2–0 lead and knocking Kaat out of the game.

Sandy was determined that two runs would be enough. He was throwing fastballs well, but as the game went on, he began losing control of his curveball. Sandy found himself in trouble in the bottom of the fifth inning. Frank Quilici started a one-out rally with a double, then Sandy walked pinch hitter Rich Rollins.

Dodger broadcaster Vin Scully was worried about Sandy's sudden inability to throw his curveball for strikes. "Koufax is struggling," he said. "It's almost impossible to [win] on one pitch in the big leagues, and he does not have a curveball [today]."

With runners on first and second and one out, Sandy faced Versalles. He got ahead in the count, 1–2, but Versalles ripped the next pitch down the third-base line. At first, it looked like a sure double that would tie the game. But third baseman Jim Gilliam made a great backhanded stab, then rolled to third base for the inning's second out. Koufax later called it the play of the game. He got the next batter, Joe Nossek, to ground out. The lead was safe.

Sandy continued to put down the Twins' hitters. Inning after inning passed with no change to the score. Finally, it was the bottom of the ninth. Sandy needed just three more outs to give the Dodgers a World Series championship. But it wouldn't be easy—he was facing the heart of the Twins' powerful lineup. First up was Tony Oliva, considered by many to be one of the greatest pure hitters the game has ever seen. On an 0–2 count, Oliva had to take a defensive swing and grounded out to third base.

Next up was Harmon Killebrew, a future Hall of Famer. Killebrew lined a sharp single to left field—just the third hit of the day for the Twins. With a runner on, one swing of the bat could tie the game. Drysdale was warming up again, ready to come in if Sandy showed any more signs of fatigue.

Battey stepped up, eager for a chance to be the hero. Sandy delivered three fastballs, all of them strikes. He was one out away.

Bob Allison, whose home run the day before had sealed the Twins' victory, was all that stood between Sandy and a game-seven shutout. Sandy kept going to his best pitch—the fastball. After four pitches, the count was 2–2. Allison was down to his last strike.

Sandy took a deep breath and prepared to deliver his 107th pitch of the day—another fastball. Allison took a mighty swing and missed. The game was over. Sandy had his second shutout in three days, and the Dodgers were the World Series champions.

It was possibly the greatest achievement of Sandy Koufax's incredible career. He was at the height of his dominance. As he celebrated with his teammates, he savored every moment, knowing that his amazing left arm might not hold up for many more seasons.

Chapter One

Brooklyn Born

Sanford Braun was born in the Borough Park section of Brooklyn, New York, on December 30, 1935. His parents, Jack and Evelyn, lived in a Jewish part of the crowded middle-class neighborhood. But when Sandy was three, his father divorced his mother and abandoned them. Evelyn had to move in with her parents. She worked long hours as an accountant to support the little family, so Sandy spent much of his time with his grandparents, Max and Dora.

Max had a big influence on Sandy. A devoted Jew, he instilled a sense of cultural pride in his grandson. He taught Sandy about music and theater and saw to the boy's religious upbringing. The pair also had fun, often going to the beach at Coney Island to swim in the ocean.

At an early age, Sandy showed that he was an athlete. He loved almost any kind of sport and spent hours playing punchball and stickball (variations of baseball) in the streets of Brooklyn. He watched the Brooklyn Dodgers play baseball at nearby Ebbets Field. Although Sandy was intelligent, he didn't always have a sharp interest in school. He'd rather be outside playing than inside doing homework.

When Sandy was nine, his mother married a lawyer named Irving Koufax. Sandy took his new father's last name. Together, the new family moved to Long Island's Rockville Centre, a suburb of New York City. Sandy's new home was vastly different from his old one. Out of the city and into the suburbs, he was surrounded by more parks and open space than he'd ever known in Brooklyn.

Sandy quickly grew close to his new stepfather. "When I speak of my father," Sandy later wrote, "I speak of Irving Koufax, for he has been to me everything a father could be."

 When Sandy's mom remarried, Sandy got a stepsister, Edie.

Sandy attended the Morris School, where he was a star athlete, playing football, basketball, and baseball. He was named the school's Athlete of the Year twice.

In 1950, after Sandy finished ninth grade, the family moved back to Brooklyn to be closer to Manhattan, where Irving and Evelyn worked. There, Sandy spent much of his time at the local Jewish Community House (JCH). The building housed a basketball court, swimming pool, weight room, and more. It was the perfect hangout for a young athlete like Sandy.

That fall, fourteen-year-old Sandy started the tenth grade at Lafayette High School. He quickly made his mark there as a star athlete, but his sport was basketball, not baseball. Everything in Sandy's life took a backseat to playing basketball.

❝ *I played baseball mainly because I had nothing to do. My friends played, so I played.*❞

—SANDY KOUFAX

Bold on the basketball court, Sandy was quiet but friendly off it. A friend remembered him as a teenager. "The other guys were so noisy," she said. "[Sandy] radiated a presence. Even as a child, he had that. His shyness filled the room."

Sandy's athletic career was thrown off track in the spring of 1951, when a coaches' strike shut down the athletics program at Lafayette. To fill the void, the six-foot-two teenager spent his time at the JCH. There, he led their basketball team to the Jewish Welfare Board championship. "This guy was a world-class athlete at the age of seventeen," said Milt Gold, the director of athletics at JCH.

Although basketball was his first passion, Sandy also enjoyed playing baseball. But he wasn't known as a pitcher yet—instead, he played mainly first base. His teammates noticed his strong arm but also saw that he wasn't much of a hitter.

Fred Wilpon, one of Sandy's friends, was the baseball star. He was good enough that the Dodgers were offering him a contract. By contrast, Sandy barely got noticed. But that was okay with him. His dreams weren't of playing for the Dodgers—he wanted to be a National Basketball Association (NBA) star for the New York Knicks.

NEW YORK KNICKERBOCKERS

The New York Knickerbockers—also known as the Knicks—were founded in 1946. Knickerbockers were a style of pants worn by Dutch settlers in New York City in the 1600s. The name has been associated with sports since 1845, when the first organized baseball team was called the Knickerbockers. The Knickerbockers often practiced and played in Hoboken, New Jersey. But by the early 1870s, the baseball team had dissolved.

By his senior year, Sandy was the captain of Lafayette's basketball team. In February 1953, Lafayette scheduled a scrimmage (practice game) with a team featuring several members of the Knicks. Among the players to attend was Harry Gallatin, one of Sandy's heroes.

Before the game, Gallatin tried to put on a dunking show for the crowd. But he failed on both dunks he tried. Lafayette's basketball coach teased the pro, telling him that one of his players would show him how to dunk. He called Sandy over, and the eighteen-year-old threw down a couple of effortless dunks, to the crowd's great delight.

During the scrimmage, most of the professional players were just goofing around. But not Sandy. He was playing the best he could, eager to prove himself against the NBA stars. Soon, Gallatin realized that he was being embarrassed by the youngster. "We just wanted to have fun," Gallatin said. "Koufax didn't want to have fun."

After the scrimmage, the *New York Post* gave Sandy his first newspaper headline: "Lafayette Cager Wowed Gallatin." *Cager* was slang for basketball player. By this point, it was easy to believe that Sandy might have a future as a professional athlete. .But nobody would have guessed that it would be as a baseball player. In fact, Sandy didn't even make the Lafayette baseball team until the spring of 1953—his senior year.

During one of Sandy's high school baseball games, Milt Laurie saw him play. Laurie managed a sandlot team called the Parkviews, and he asked Koufax to play for the team. Sandlot teams played in loosely organized leagues on small fields called sandlots. Laurie wanted to try the strong lefty as a pitcher. Sandy had a blazing fastball, but he was wild. Most of the hitters who faced him either struck out or walked. But when Sandy was on, he was devastating. He threw a no-hitter in one of his first games for the team and quickly became the team's best pitcher. Before long, major league scouts were watching him.

NO-HITTERS AND PERFECT GAMES

Sometimes called the "no-no," the no-hitter is an achievement every starting pitcher strives for. In a no-hitter, the pitcher does not allow any official hits. A batter can get on base (and even score) only by being hit by a pitch, by being walked, or by a fielding error. For a pitcher, the only thing better than throwing a no-hitter is throwing a perfect game. A perfect game is just as it sounds—perfect. A pitcher throws a complete game without allowing a single base runner. In a nine-inning game, a pitcher must face twenty-seven batters and retire all twenty-seven in order. It's one of the rarest accomplishments in baseball.

"One time when Koufax pitched, the entire infield and outfield sat down," said a teammate. "He only walked people or struck them out."

Major league teams are always interested in a left-handed pitcher who can throw hard—a fact as true in the 1950s as it is in the early 2000s. Because hard-throwing lefties are so rare, Sandy could have probably signed a minor league contract right out of high school. But his parents had stressed the importance of education, and he was determined to go to college. He knew that in college, he'd be able to play baseball as well as basketball— still his first love. He also hoped to earn a degree and become an architect.

Sandy had seen the University of Cincinnati Bearcats basketball team play a game in New York's Madison Square Garden. He liked the team and decided to go to college there. Cincinnati later offered Sandy an athletic scholarship, and he was off to Ohio. Life would be very different from his time in Brooklyn, but as long as he had basketball, Sandy knew he'd be just fine.

Chapter Two

Bearcat Sensation

In the fall of 1953, seventeen-year-old Sandy Koufax enrolled in the school of liberal arts at the University of Cincinnati. He quickly got down to studying, knowing that he'd have to work hard to reach his goal of becoming an architect. Cincinnati had a work-study program in which students could alternate eight weeks of school with eight weeks of work. It was a good system for Sandy, who often had trouble focusing on his studies. His friends would later remember that he rarely put in the studying time he needed but still managed to get by on his intelligence.

Sandy started his athletic career at Cincinnati as a forward on the freshman basketball team. At the time, many colleges had separate teams for first-year students. They didn't let the freshmen compete with the upperclassmen, who played on the varsity team.

"He had long arms and could jump," remembered his coach, Ed Jucker. "He was . . . an intense player, and he had the motivation to do well. You have those ingredients, that motivation, that ability that he had, and the kind of person he was, why, he couldn't lose."

Jucker was right—Sandy did perform well for the freshman team. He averaged 9.7 points per game and helped lead the team to a 12–2 record. It was a good season, but Sandy still dreamed of playing with the upperclassmen.

Unlike in basketball, freshmen on Cincinnati's baseball team were allowed to compete in some games with the varsity team. This was welcome news for Sandy, who had recently celebrated his eighteenth birthday. The thought of playing against the best was exciting. He asked Jucker if he could join the team as a pitcher for a trip to New Orleans, Louisiana, over spring break in 1954. At first, the coach wasn't sure he believed that Sandy belonged on the baseball team. He told him to come to tryouts like everyone else.

Along with the team's other hopeful pitchers and catchers, Sandy crowded into a small, dimly lit gymnasium. When his turn finally came, he looked at his catcher and fired his hardest fastball. The ball popped loudly in the mitt, and the catcher quickly stood up and left. He didn't want to catch any more of Sandy's pitches. It hurt too much.

"The gym was dark and there was no catcher who wanted to handle his speedball," Jucker said. "He had a terrific curve too. It went straight down, and with speed. . . . It's like a revelation to see someone throw the ball that fast."

Sandy's lack of a catching partner became a problem. Some players hid in the locker room to avoid the job. Two of the team's catchers simply quit. Finally, a farm boy named Danny Gilbert offered to be Sandy's catcher (using a heavily padded mitt). The offer earned Gilbert a spot on the team alongside his hard-throwing pitcher. Gilbert later compared catching Sandy's pitches to being hit in the mitt with a sledgehammer.

66*Anyone who tried to catch him, they were just a series of bruises all over their backs, their behinds, the backs of their legs from the ball hitting the floor and tile wall and bouncing back.*99
—DON NESBITT, WHO TRIED OUT ALONGSIDE SANDY FOR THE CINCINNATI BASEBALL TEAM IN 1954

Jucker wasted little time getting Sandy into a game. Although Sandy was still wild, his amazing fastball and good curveball began to attract a lot of attention from other teams. Hitters feared him. Scouts from the major leagues wanted to see what all the fuss was about.

One day a scout from the Cincinnati Reds came to see the young lefty. Sandy was starting against Xavier, a Catholic university from across town. But he didn't tell anyone that he'd hurt his ankle tripping on a flight of stairs the night before. The sore ankle affected his delivery, and he struggled more than usual with his control. At one point, he became so upset that he blew up at the umpire—an unusual outburst from the normally quiet eighteen-year-old. The Reds' scout was understandably unimpressed. He told Jucker after the game that Sandy would never make it as a big leaguer.

Despite that difficult game, Sandy's short time with the Bearcats' baseball team was successful. He went 3–1 with a very good earned run average (ERA) of 2.81 (the average number of earned runs he gave up every nine innings). He also struck out 51 batters in just 32 innings of work.

The scout from Cincinnati wasn't the only one who had seen Sandy pitch that spring. Bill Zinser of the Brooklyn Dodgers had been left with a much better impression. Zinser rated Sandy's arm as an A+, which meant that the quality of his arm was better than most major leaguers'. But he gave Sandy a lower grade for his control. In that department, Sandy was at the level of a minor leaguer. Still, Zinser felt coaches could work with Sandy on the control. He sent the Dodgers a glowing report, saying Sandy was an excellent prospect.

After the school year, Sandy returned home and got a job as a camp counselor at Camp Chi-Wan-Da in New York. He returned to playing sandlot baseball as well and continued to amaze those who came to see him.

Meanwhile, more major league teams were giving him a close look. The New York Yankees sent a scout and offered him a minor league contract, but Sandy wasn't happy with their offer of $4,000. The New York Giants brought him in for a workout, but Sandy forgot to bring his glove and was especially wild, throwing several pitches over the catcher's head.

THE AMATEUR DRAFT

In 1965 Major League Baseball instituted the amateur draft. It replaced the old system in which teams simply signed whatever young talent they wanted and ended the days of the bonus babies. A bonus baby was a player who received a signing bonus of more than $4,000. The draft allowed teams to select amateur players in an orderly fashion, with the teams having the worst record in the previous year getting the earliest picks. It ensured that every team would have the chance to sign young talent.

The two teams that showed the most interest were the Dodgers and the Pittsburgh Pirates. During his workout with the

Pirates, Sandy threw so hard that he actually broke the thumb of bullpen coach Sam Narron, who was catching. Narron may not have been happy about it, but team officials were impressed. "That's the greatest arm I've ever seen," said Branch Rickey, the Pirates' general manager.

The Dodgers were similarly impressed. Head scout Al Campanis said of Sandy's workout, "I'll always remember that first pitch. It was a fastball that looked like it would hit the dirt in front of the plate. Then, all of a sudden, it rose for a knee-high strike. As soon as I saw that fastball, the hair raised up on my arms."

In the end, the Dodgers were the first to offer Sandy a big contract. He would receive $6,000 for his first year, with a signing bonus of $14,000. Sandy didn't sign right away, but he and his dad agreed that they would accept the offer. Soon after Sandy met with Dodger officials, a member of the Pirates front office told Sandy they'd pay $5,000 more than whatever the Dodgers were offering. The Milwaukee Braves later offered him $30,000. But Sandy and his dad said no. They'd made their deal, and they were going to stick to it.

"I had no idea about the money," Sandy said. "My father, an attorney, didn't either. What we wanted was enough money to send me back to college if I couldn't make it in baseball."

Sandy finally signed the contract in December 1954. College was still important to him, but the Dodgers told him he could attend classes during the off-season. Signing with the Dodgers would also mean his basketball career was over, but it was an easy decision. Twenty thousand dollars was a lot of money—more than Sandy could afford to turn down.

BEARCATS ON TOP

Cincinnati's men's basketball team did well when Sandy attended the school. But the team really took off shortly after he left. The Bearcats went to five straight Final Four playoff appearances beginning in 1959, and the team won the National Collegiate Athletic Association (NCAA) championship in 1961 and 1962.

Because of his big signing bonus, Sandy was guaranteed a spot on the Dodgers' twenty-five-man roster. Major League Baseball had recently passed a rule stating that any player receiving a bonus of more than $4,000 had to remain on the big league roster for a minimum of two seasons. The rule had been passed to stop teams from buying all the young talent they could find and then leaving them in the minor leagues for years and years.

In less than a year, Sandy had gone from a college basketball player who had decided to try out for his school's baseball team to a member of the Brooklyn Dodgers. He wouldn't even be making a stop in the minor leagues first.

 Because Sandy had been guaranteed a roster spot in 1955, the Dodgers had to send another player down to the minor leagues. That player was Tommy Lasorda, a longtime minor league pitcher and future Dodger manager.

Not everyone was happy with the signing. Some Dodger players and coaches complained that the youngster would be wasting a valuable roster spot. Sandy was still wild, and many coaches and players felt that he had nothing to contribute. But for better or worse, Sandy was a Dodger.

Chapter | Three

Bonus Baby

Sandy had always been in great shape. He was tall and muscular, with strong, wide shoulders, a broad chest, and powerful legs. But when he arrived for spring training camp in Vero Beach, Florida, in the spring of 1955 (a week earlier than pitchers were required to report), he quickly learned that he'd have to take fitness to a new level. The coaching staff didn't rush him into pitching instruction as he'd expected. Instead, it was all about physical conditioning. In those first days of camp, Sandy *ran*.

Walter Alston was beginning his second year as the Dodger manager. The team and its fans were hungry for a World Series title, having lost five World Series in the past fifteen years. But in 1955, they came in with a powerful lineup and a real chance to finally win a championship. Few people took notice of the new "bonus baby." The *New York Times* even called

21

him "the bonus right-hander." Sandy would have to earn his respect here.

Spring training officially began on March 1, 1955. Sandy quickly lived up to his reputation as a wild thrower. Wearing a Dodger uniform with the number 32 on his back, Sandy sailed his first pitch over the screen behind home plate and onto the roof of the press box behind it. Sandy later admitted that he was totally lost. Baseball had never been his game, and he couldn't keep up with everything going on around him. "I was so scared," he said of the experience.

The coaches worked with Sandy on his motion and delivery, helping him learn the proper mechanics for pitching. Unlike many pitchers, who throw with their arms at an angle (often called a three-quarter angle), Sandy's delivery was almost straight up and down. This style—combined with his powerful, athletic build and his high leg kick—was the reason his pitches had such amazing speed. But it also reduced the amount of movement he could get on his pitches, especially side-to-side movement. Sandy threw a 12-to-6 curveball, so named because the path of the ball goes straight down, like tracing from the number twelve down to the six on the face of a clock.

Another problem that coaches tried to help Sandy solve was his tendency to tip his pitches. His windup and delivery weren't the same for each type of pitch, and observant hitters could figure out what he was going to throw before he actually released the ball. The coaches helped him as much as they could, but it was a problem that Sandy would never completely solve. Even in his finest years, hitters around the National League (NL) still could read what was coming.

The Dodgers business office was thrilled to have Sandy, a Brooklyn Jew, on the team. Brooklyn had a big Jewish population, and the Dodgers hoped that having Sandy on the roster would help attract more Jewish fans to the ballpark.

Just before spring training ended, the Dodgers played a game against the Dodgertown All-Stars. The team was made up of the Dodgers' best minor leaguers and was just a final tune-up game before the regular season. Alston didn't want to use one of his regular starters, so he picked Sandy to start the game. Sandy did a good job against the minor leaguers, striking out five hitters in three innings. But he also knew that such chances would be few and far between once the season began.

The Dodgers started the regular season with a bang, winning their first ten games and twenty-two of their first twenty-four. The team took off to a huge lead in the NL standings. But

Sandy could only watch. He was on the disabled list (DL) with a hairline fracture in his ankle. According to the team, he had suffered the injury when he stepped on a sprinkler during warm-ups. But it's far more likely that the injury was made up to free a roster spot for a pitcher that the Dodgers believed was more ready to contribute.

"He had great stuff and you could see he had great potential," said teammate Ed Roebuck. "Because of the bonus rule, he couldn't be sent down [to the minors]. So it was a very bad situation for him because he should have been in the minor leagues developing rather than sitting around at that level."

After thirty days, Sandy finally came off the DL and was placed on the active roster (Tommy Lasorda, his replacement, had been 0–4 and was sent down to the minors). Two weeks later, on June 24, Sandy finally got his first chance to pitch.

The Dodgers were in Milwaukee, Wisconsin, playing the Braves. (The Braves played in Milwaukee from 1953 until 1965, when the team moved to Atlanta, Georgia.) They trailed 7–1 in the fifth inning, and Alston needed a fresh arm. It was the perfect time to get a look at the bonus baby. The game was already getting out of hand, so even if Sandy couldn't throw a strike, it wouldn't get much worse.

Sandy walked slowly to the mound in front of more than 43,000 excited and noisy Braves fans. After waiting and watching through sixty-six games, Sandy was finally getting his chance. The first batter he faced was shortstop Johnny Logan. Sandy calmed himself and delivered his first big-league pitch. Logan watched it sail by, and the umpire called, "Strike!" But the next two pitches were balls. On the 2–1 count, Logan finally took a swing and looped a single into shallow right field. It was a weakly hit ball, but it still counted as a hit.

The next hitter, Eddie Mathews, bunted. It was a poor bunt that rolled right back to Sandy. All he had to do was turn and throw to second base to start an easy double play. But instead of getting two outs, Sandy threw wildly into center field. Both runners were safe.

A FRIEND TO ALL

Early in his career, Sandy earned a reputation as being a friend to African American players as well as to whites. Because of his Jewish heritage, he knew what prejudice felt like. In a time when teammates of different races often didn't socialize with one another, Sandy was friendly with all of his teammates.

With runners at first and second and nobody out, Sandy was in trouble. Hank Aaron, who would go on to become the most prolific home run hitter in major league history, stepped up to the plate. Trying to be careful with the slugger, Sandy walked him on four pitches. Now the bases were loaded with nobody out. Sandy's first appearance was looking like a disaster.

Bobby Thompson was up next. Sandy fell behind in the count 2–0, but he came back to run the count full (three balls and two strikes). On the next pitch, he threw a hard fastball past the swinging Thompson—strike three!

Sandy had his first big-league strikeout, but he still had the bases loaded with only one out. He got the next hitter, Joe Adcock, to hit a ground ball to the shortstop, who flipped the ball to the second baseman to start an inning-ending double play. Somehow, Sandy had gotten out of the inning without giving up a run. He also pitched a scoreless sixth inning for a successful— though tense—major league debut. Even though the Dodgers lost the game 8–2, Sandy had to feel good about his performance.

Five days later, Sandy got his next chance to pitch in a similar situation—and with eerily similar results. With the Dodgers trailing the Giants 6–0, Sandy came in to pitch the ninth inning. Alvin Dark led off the inning with a single, then Whitey Lockman reached base on a bunt. Again, Sandy faced a future Hall of Famer, Willie Mays, with two runners on and nobody out. And again, Sandy issued a walk to load the bases. It was almost a replay of his first outing. And just as he had against the

Braves, Sandy got out of trouble without allowing a run, getting two fly outs and a groundout that ended the inning.

It was far from an ideal start, but the Dodger coaches were impressed with the nineteen-year-old's ability to get out of a jam. A week later (July 6), against the Pittsburgh Pirates, the coaches rewarded Sandy with his first big-league start.

At first, Sandy's performance was all too familiar. He walked three of his first four hitters in the first inning. But again, he escaped the inning without giving up a run. Through four innings, he'd allowed just one hit, although he'd issued six walks.

In the fifth inning, Sandy finally got into a situation that he couldn't get out of. He walked two more batters and then gave up two singles. Alston pulled him out of the game one pitch (a ball) later. In four and two-thirds innings, Sandy had surrendered 3 hits, 8 walks, and 1 run. He'd also recorded 4 strikeouts. In total, he threw 105 pitches (52 strikes and 53 balls)—a very high total for less than five innings of work. The Dodgers lost the game 4–1.

The coaches had their doubts about their bonus baby. Sandy barely played over the next seven weeks, seeing only three short relief appearances during that time. Because he couldn't be sent to the minors, Sandy was wasting away on the bench. He wasn't good enough to put into a close game, and he couldn't get better without a chance to pitch.

In the third of those relief appearances, Sandy pitched the last inning of a game against the Cincinnati Reds—one of the better hitting teams in the National League. He started the inning by striking out his first two batters on six straight strikes, then struck out the third hitter as well. Alston was impressed. He decided to give Sandy another shot at starting. The Dodgers had a big lead in the NL standings, so Alston could afford to take another chance on the nineteen-year-old.

When Alston informed Jake Pitler that Sandy was going to get his second career start, the Dodger first-base coach reportedly replied, "Oh, no."

On August 27, Sandy took the mound for his second career start—against the Reds. Unlike his first start, this was a home game for the Dodgers. Sandy's friends and family filled the stands, cheering loudly. After giving up a first-inning single to Ted Kluszewski, Sandy's pitching was close to perfect. His fastball was humming and his curve was confusing hitters and forcing them into bad swings. Most important, Sandy was in total command. His wildness had disappeared, at least for a day. After striking out one hitter in the first inning, he struck out two in each of the next two innings. He added one strikeout in the fourth, two in the fifth, and another in the sixth. By the end of the seventh inning, his strikeout total had climbed to eleven.

Although his arm was tiring and he was starting to lose control of his curveball, Sandy was having a blast and wasn't about to come out of the ballgame. He got his twelfth and thirteenth strikeouts in the eighth inning and added one more in the ninth, helping to seal a shutout win. Fourteen strikeouts in one game—it was the highest total for any NL pitcher that year. And it came from a nineteen-year-old rookie whose own coaches barely trusted him.

Sandy's first major league win made headlines. A two-hit, fourteen-strikeout shutout against a hard-hitting team would have been big news for any pitcher, but coming from Sandy, it was the talk of Brooklyn.

"Every pitch was *whomp, whomp, whomp,*" said one of the Reds' pitchers after watching Sandy pitch. "Next day, [our manager] says, 'That rookie made us look terrible. Where the [heck] they been keeping him?'"

After giving up several hard hits in a relief appearance, Sandy got another start a week later. Although his performance wasn't as exciting as the fourteen-strikeout game had been, he still pitched a fantastic game. He walked only two Pittsburgh Pirates while striking out six, and he got his second career victory—again by shutout. By this time, the Dodgers coaches never knew what to expect out of Sandy. He could look like the best pitcher on the team one day and like a bad minor leaguer the next.

Sandy pitched only twice more after that, both times in relief. He lost both games and finished 1955 with a 2–2 record and a solid 3.02 ERA.

Meanwhile, the Dodgers clinched the NL pennant and faced the Yankees in the World Series. Sandy never got to play in the series, but he was with the team as they finally broke through and beat New York in seven games.

After the 1955 season, Sandy enrolled in Columbia University. But classes overlapped with the team's World Series victory party. Sandy had to ask permission from his professor to miss class and go to the party.

Despite remaining on the bench, just being on the roster exposed Sandy to baseball's Fall Classic and all of the media that surrounds the event. And because he was on the roster, Sandy got a nice World Series bonus of $9,768.21. Ironically, the bonus almost completely made up for the extra money he had turned down from the Braves just a year before. Sandy's big-league career was off to quite a start.

Chapter | Four

Watching and Waiting

Despite his scattered success in 1955, Sandy still wasn't confident that he could make a living as a ballplayer. He continued to take classes at Columbia University during the off-season. If baseball didn't work out—as it didn't for so many bonus babies—he intended to have a good fallback plan.

When he headed to Vero Beach in the spring of 1956, Sandy knew that he was probably facing a season much like the one he'd just endured. Little had changed—Sandy still lacked experience and consistency, the Dodgers would still be in a pennant race, and Walter Alston would still be reluctant to use the twenty-year-old. Sandy figured that he was in for another long season of watching and waiting.

"I missed that training, that experience a young pitcher needs," Sandy later said of his situation. "A couple of seasons in the minor leagues would probably have solved my control problem, and I might have been ready to win in the National League three or four years before I finally found myself."

In 1956 the Dodgers had another hot young pitcher to go along with Sandy. Don Drysdale, a nineteen-year-old right-hander from California, joined the staff. Although Drysdale was a rookie and Sandy was in his second year, Alston had a lot more trust in the righty. Sandy had to watch from the bench as Drysdale got the regular work any young pitcher needs to develop.

When Sandy did get a chance to pitch, Alston would give him almost no room for error. If he gave up a hit or walked a batter, the manager would often have someone start warming up in the bullpen. Nobody can pitch error-free baseball, especially an inexperienced twenty-year-old. All that added pressure couldn't have helped Sandy's confidence.

In one game, Sandy got to start when Drysdale had a sore arm. But despite six fairly good innings, Alston pulled Sandy out of the game in the seventh—and the Dodgers went on to lose. In another start, Sandy had given up just one run through three innings. But when he started the fourth inning with a walk and reached a 2–0 count on the next hitter, Alston again pulled him out of the game. Any other pitcher on the staff would have been given the chance to pitch out of the situation. But not Sandy.

While Alston had no faith in his young lefty, some of his teammates were beginning to warm up to him. Jackie Robinson, famous for being the first African American to break the color barrier in the major leagues, argued with Alston over the way he used (or didn't use) Sandy. Robinson believed that Sandy had talent, and he didn't like to see it wasted on the bench.

From his first year on, Sandy had the Dodgers arrange his pitching schedule so that he could observe the major Jewish holidays with prayer. He often went home to spend those days with his parents.

Before long, reporters were asking similar questions. After all, hadn't Sandy struck out fourteen batters in a game? Hadn't he pitched two complete-game shutouts (games in which he pitched all nine innings and the opposing team didn't score any runs)? That was quite a feat for a teenager—shouldn't that talent be allowed to develop?

In June a reporter from the *Daily News* wrote an article about Sandy that was very critical of Alston. He wrote: "For some reason that escapes me, Alston manifests very little confidence in Koufax. A pitching pinch has to develop before Walt uses the kid. Then, it seems, Sandy must pitch a shutout or the bullpen is working full force and the kid will be yanked at the first long foul ball."

Despite growing criticism, Alston was set in his ways. So Sandy sat on the bench, rarely getting the chance to pitch.

Another new addition to the 1956 Dodgers was veteran right-hander Sal Maglie. The thirty-nine-year-old played an important role as a starting pitcher for the Dodgers, but he also spent time working with the organization's young pitchers—especially Sandy. He taught Sandy about setting up hitters—not always throwing hard, but thinking about how to keep them off balance. Maglie's career was winding down, but he was happy to share his knowledge, and Sandy was happy to learn all that he could.

❝ If [Sandy] got in the groove early, he was awesome. He was just not polished or refined enough to be consistent. . . . He had spurts [of greatness] in those early years, and that's why [the Dodgers] stayed with him. ❞

—TEAMMATE CARL ERSKINE

In total Sandy pitched in 16 games that year, totaling 58⅔ innings. It was more work than he'd gotten in 1955, but not by much. And his performance was worse—he finished the year with a 2–4 record and a high ERA of 4.91. He struck out 30 batters while walking 29. If Sandy's confidence had been low before the season, it was only lower afterward.

Despite Sandy's struggles, the Dodgers again won the NL pennant in a close race over the Braves. The 1956 World Series was a rematch of the previous year—Dodgers versus Yankees. But this time, the Yankees prevailed in seven games. Once again, Sandy never got to pitch in the series. Drysdale, meanwhile, pitched two innings of relief.

Sandy desperately needed the opportunity to pitch, so the Dodgers sent him to play winter ball in Puerto Rico. Winter ball gave many young major and minor league players the chance to get extra instruction and hone their skills. In Puerto Rico, Sandy finally got a chance to pitch regularly. He worked on controlling both his fastball and his curveball. One day, his teammates even tried to teach him how to throw a spitball. To throw a spitball, a pitcher applies a small amount of saliva to the ball to affect its spin. It's an illegal pitch in the modern game, but it was common at the time. Sandy, however, got it all wrong, applying way too much saliva to the ball, and promptly decided that the spitter wasn't for him.

Sandy returned for the 1957 season, which began very much like the previous two years had. Because he had spent thirty days on the DL in 1955, he still had to remain on Brooklyn's roster for thirty days in 1957. After that time, the

Dodgers would finally be free to send him down to the minor leagues.

Still, sitting on the bench for most of that month was frustrating for Sandy. He had been throwing well during spring training and felt that he was ready to contribute to the team.

On May 15, Sandy's two years on the Dodgers' roster were up. But before sending him to the minors, Alston decided to give the twenty-one-year-old lefty one last shot.

Sandy was pitching for his job when he took the mound at Chicago's Wrigley Field to face the Cubs on May 16. Would this be the wild Sandy Koufax fans had seen in 1956? Or would it be the Sandy Koufax who had hurled two shutouts as a rookie? Sandy gave Dodger fans the answer they wanted, striking out thirteen Cubs and getting a 3–2, complete-game victory. Suddenly, the team's plans changed. Not only did Alston decide not to send Sandy to the minor leagues, he gave him a spot in the starting rotation!

Sandy won two of his next four starts. He was still wild at times, but he was becoming a more and more effective pitcher.

On June 4, Sandy faced the Cubs again. As he had before, he showed Dodger fans that he really did belong in the majors. He struck out six of his first eight batters. By the fourth inning, radio broadcaster Vin Scully was gushing over the young lefty. "Koufax is remarkable with his strikeouts this year," Scully said.

"If you figure out how many innings he's pitched and how many strikeouts he has, you really start to shake your head."

Sandy carried a no-hitter into the sixth inning and struck out twelve batters before tiring and coming out of the game in the seventh. The Dodgers went on to win the game, 7–5.

❝ *[Koufax] couldn't cope with mediocrity. He wouldn't stand for it.* **❞**

—TEAMMATE ED ROEBUCK

His performance gave Sandy a total of 59 strikeouts in the season—more than any other NL pitcher at that point. And he'd done it in less than 50 innings of work! In addition, he had lowered his ERA to 2.90, which ranked twelfth among NL pitchers. Sandy was pitching great, and he had the statistics to prove it.

Inexplicably, Sandy didn't get another start for a month and a half. He returned to his role of sitting on the bench, watching and waiting and wondering what he had to do to stay in the starting rotation.

By this time, Sandy had the confidence of most of his teammates, many of whom were furious with the way he was being treated. Star shortstop Harold "Pee Wee" Reese clashed with Alston over the issue. Longtime Dodger Danny Ozark suggested that someone in the organization was intentionally holding Sandy back.

"I know [Sandy] was upset," Ozark later said. "They could have given him a chance to pitch, especially in '57. . . . Somebody upstairs had a reason for this. It has to go back to the [general manager]."

When Sandy did finally get another start on July 19, he pitched well, striking out eleven. But whatever momentum he'd built in March and early June was long gone. He struggled down the stretch, winning only one more game after his June 4 gem against the Cubs. He finished the year at 5–4 (his first winning record) and with a respectable 3.88 ERA. In 104 innings of work, he had walked 51 while striking out 122.

Statistically, it was a good year for Sandy. But for Brooklyn baseball fans, it ended as a nightmare. After the Dodgers finished in third place in the National League, eleven games behind the Braves, owner Walter O'Malley announced that the team was leaving Brooklyn. Beginning in 1958, the club would be known as the Los Angeles Dodgers. Fittingly, Sandy—born and raised in Brooklyn—was the last man to throw a pitch for the Brooklyn Dodgers.

Chapter Five

Struggles in the Sunshine State

Everything was changing in 1958. The Dodger organization moved across the country to a new ballpark and new fans. The core of players that had led the team to the World Series in 1955 and 1956—Robinson, Reese, Don Newcombe, and others—was no longer together. (Robinson and Reese retired, and Newcombe was traded to the Reds.) Worse still, the team's star catcher, Roy Campanella, had been paralyzed in a January car accident. But despite it all, baseball went on.

Sandy shared a Los Angeles apartment with catcher and fellow Brooklyn native Joe Pignatano. They quickly discovered that life in Los Angeles was a lot different from life in Brooklyn. Girls were always chasing the young, single players, and Sandy didn't know how to handle all of the attention. He dated but never really got serious with anyone. He was content to focus on his baseball career for a while.

The first game in the Dodgers' new home—Los Angeles Memorial Coliseum—was played on April 18, 1958. More than 78,000 fans filled the enormous stadium, which had been used for the 1932 Olympics. The Coliseum was vastly different from Brooklyn's cozy Ebbets Field, a stadium with small dimensions that favored hard-hitting teams. The Coliseum, by comparison, was a pitcher's paradise. The outfield fence was as far as 440 feet from home plate in some spots, making home runs few and far between. Down the left-field line, the fence was only 251 feet away, but a 40-foot screen above it protected a pitcher against easy homers.

The Dodgers' opponent in the first game was the San Francisco Giants. Like the Dodgers, the Giants had just moved from New York to California. The Giants won that opening game 8–0, but the fans barely cared. They were just thrilled to have major league baseball in the Golden State.

Despite all of the changes, some things remained the same. Sandy, now twenty-two years old, still had a reputation for being wild (although some claim that by this point, that criticism wasn't entirely fair). Walter Alston remained the team's manager, and his opinion of Sandy hadn't changed.

It was a new city and a new ballpark, but for the first month of the 1958 season, Sandy found himself in a familiar place—on the bench. He saw only spot duty until May 20, when he finally made his mark. He pitched an entire eleven-inning game against the National League's best team, the Milwaukee Braves, earning a 6–3 victory—his first of the season.

---

66 *[Koufax] doesn't know what it means to pitch and win in the majors. He's got one of those silent tempers. He gets mad at himself and decides to overpower the hitter.* 99

—BUZZIE BAVASI, GENERAL MANAGER OF THE DODGERS

Sandy's situation began to brighten after that big win. He was pitching well, enjoying the spacious new ballpark, finding his control, and running his record to 7–3. It was an impressive mark, especially since the Dodgers were really struggling as a team.

But as had happened in the past, it seemed that just when things started to go Sandy's way, something got in the way of success. In a July start against the Cubs, Sandy turned his ankle while he tried to cover first base to get a force-out. He had to sit for two weeks to rest the sore ankle and was never fully able to regain his form. He went 4–8 down the stretch and struggled in several of his outings. He finished the year with a record of 11–11. His ERA of 4.48 was too high, and he walked 105 batters while striking out 131. He also led the league with 17 wild pitches (a Dodger record that still stands).

The statistics weren't great, but for the first time, Sandy had gotten consistent work. Finally, after three years of being almost an afterthought, Sandy was a real part of the team—even if it was a team that finished the season second to last in the NL standings.

Sandy's up-and-down ways continued throughout the 1959 season. In the early months, he struggled. For a time, everyone was wondering when (not if) the Dodgers would send him to the minor leagues. After spending more than four years with a big-league team, those would have been tough orders to take—maybe even tough enough to drive Sandy from the game.

"He has no coordination and he has lost all his confidence," said Joe Becker, the Dodgers pitching coach. "His arm is sound, but mechanically, he is all fouled up." Alston added, "He's either awfully good or awfully bad."

Something had changed in the Dodger clubhouse. For years, fans, reporters, and even players had begged Alston to give Sandy a chance. In 1959 when many were telling Alston to send the lefty down, he refused. "You can't give up on him," Alston insisted.

Sandy rewarded Alston's confidence by finally winning a game at the end of May. The win set him off on a small hot streak, and he won each of his next four decisions.

In late June, Sandy made headlines by striking out sixteen Philadelphia Phillies in a 6–2 win, setting a record for strikeouts in a night game. He victimized the Phillies again in late August with a thirteen-strikeout game. He wasn't always at his best, but Sandy was showing flashes of his tremendous talent.

Meanwhile, the Dodgers were again in a pennant race. The San Francisco Giants, their new California rivals, were in first place with a narrow lead over the Dodgers and Braves.

PITCH SELECTION

Sandy relied mainly on two pitches throughout his career—a four-seam fastball and a curveball. The fastball had a rising motion, while the curveball fell away from the hitter. Sandy also threw a changeup (which looks like a fastball but travels much more slowly) and a forkball (similar to a fastball but with little spin and a different movement toward the plate).

The Giants came to Los Angeles at the end of August for a big three-game series. The teams split the first two games of the series, which allowed the Giants to maintain their two-game lead over the Dodgers. With less than a month to play before the end of the season, the Dodgers couldn't afford to fall three games back. So when Sandy took the mound that Monday night before more than 82,000 fans, it was by far the biggest start of his career. Alston wasn't sure how the twenty-three-year-old lefty would respond to the pressure.

After opening the game with back-to-back strikeouts, Sandy gave up a first-inning run on two doubles. Through three innings, the score remained 1–0, and Sandy struck out only three of the batters he faced. But then, something clicked. Suddenly, Sandy was almost unhittable. He recorded strikeout after strikeout, making a good Giant lineup look almost silly at the plate. Twelve of the next fourteen outs Sandy recorded were strikeouts.

Entering the top of the ninth, Sandy had a chance to make history. The NL record for strikeouts in a game was seventeen, by Jay Hanna "Dizzy" Dean, while Bob Feller held the major league record (also the American League record) of eighteen. And if that wasn't enough pressure, the game was tied 2–2.

With a mix of hard fastballs and sinking curves, Sandy struck out the first two hitters on three pitches each. The crowd went crazy, knowing he was one strikeout away from tying Feller's mark.

Jack Sanford stepped to the plate, and Sandy used three fastballs to take a lead in the count at 1–2. He had no reason to throw anything else on the fourth pitch. Sanford swung and missed. Sandy had done it—eighteen strikeouts in a single game! He'd also set a record for the most strikeouts in back-to-back starts with thirty-one. And the day only got better in the bottom of the ninth when Wally Moon hit a three-run homer to give the Dodgers a much-needed 5–2 win.

The Los Angeles fans and media went wild. The *Los Angeles Times* called the game "one of the most momentous victories in the Dodgers' glorious history."

Indeed, it was a big win, and it propelled the Dodgers to a first-place tie with the Braves for the National League pennant. After the Dodgers swept the Braves in a best-of-three-game playoff, they headed to Chicago to face the White Sox in the 1959 World Series.

Somehow, the Dodgers had won the National League with a modest 86–68 record. In most years, a team needed at least 90 wins—and sometimes as many as 100—to clinch the title. Sandy's regular-season record was 8–6 with an improved ERA of 4.05. He'd recorded 173 strikeouts in 153⅓ innings.

Sandy got his first taste of World Series action in game one, but it wasn't the way he wanted to get in. Starting pitcher Roger Craig got hammered by the potent Chicago lineup, and the Dodgers were down 11–0 by the end of the fourth inning. With the game out of reach, Alston called the bullpen and asked for his young lefty.

Sandy did his part in the game, pitching two perfect innings, but it didn't really matter. The White Sox got an easy 11–0 win, and it looked like they might blow out the Dodgers.

Sandy was still an unknown to many baseball fans during the 1959 World Series. Broadcaster Mel Allen even mispronounced his name "KOO-fax" before game one. The correct pronunciation is KOH-fax.

But as bad as things had looked in game one, the Dodgers weren't giving up. They came back to win the next three games by a combined total of four runs and found themselves with a commanding 3–1 lead in the series.

In a surprising move, Alston chose Sandy to pitch game five. It was Sandy's chance to really contribute—a win would seal the championship for the Dodgers. He and his teammates badly wanted to win in front of the huge Coliseum crowd (the final two games were scheduled to be played in Chicago).

The game was an intense pitcher's duel between Sandy and Bob Shaw, who had gone 18–6 with a 2.69 ERA during the regular season. Entering the fourth inning, the game remained scoreless. But then Sandy found himself in trouble. He had runners at first and third with nobody out. On a hard-hit ground ball off the bat of Sherm Lollar, the Dodgers chose to take a double play instead of trying to throw out the runner at home. The run gave the White Sox a 1–0 lead.

It was the only run that Sandy gave up through seven innings (he was pulled for a pinch hitter in the bottom of the seventh), but it was enough for the White Sox. Sandy was the hard-luck loser in a 1–0 game.

Sandy's dejection didn't last long, though. Two days later, Los Angeles beat the White Sox 9–3 to win the World Series. After only two years, the Dodgers were bringing a championship home to California.

As high as Sandy must have felt to have been playing for—and contributing to—a championship, those good feelings quickly faded in 1960. He was pitching worse than ever. His control was terrible, and he couldn't seem to get anybody out. And again, he wasn't getting regular work. After five long years, his frustration had reached a boiling point. He lashed out at Dodgers general manager Buzzie Bavasi, demanding that the Dodgers either play him or trade him.

"I had a lot of faults," Sandy later admitted. "I'd get mad at myself every time I made a mistake, and it seemed like I made a mistake every time I threw the ball. So then I'd try to throw a little harder, and I'd get a little wilder, and then I'd finally get the ball over, and they'd get a hit."

As the season dragged on, the situation didn't get any better. Sandy would be good one day, then terrible the next. His highlight of the year was a one-hit shutout of the Pirates. But it was overshadowed by many more bad days. By June, his record was a horrible 1–8. Although he rebounded a bit in the second half of the year, it was still a failure. His record of 8–13 was the worst of his career, even though his ERA dropped to 3.91 and his 197 strikeouts were second most in the league (only Drysdale had more).

After the season, Sandy seriously thought about quitting baseball. He'd been at it for six years, and he didn't feel like he was getting any better. In some ways, he felt like he was getting worse. After the last game of the season, he threw all of his equipment in a garbage can. In his frustration, he'd decided that he wouldn't need it anymore. Nobe Kawano, a clubhouse worker who saw him do it, told him, "If you want to quit, go ahead. But I wish you'd leave your arm." Kawano then dug out the equipment and packed it away so it would be waiting for Sandy the next spring.

In the end, Sandy decided that he owed the Dodgers one more shot. He told himself that he would go to spring training the following year, giving his every effort to improve. But if things still weren't working out when the season began, then he would retire and find something else to do with his life.

Chapter Six

Turning the Corner

During the off-season, Sandy worked with pitching coach Joe Becker. Together, they made small adjustments to his delivery as well as his grip on his curveball. They hoped these small changes would improve Sandy's control, give him a better break on his curveball, and reduce his problem of tipping his pitches to the batter.

Sandy got more help during spring training, but this time, it came from an unexpected source—backup catcher Norm Sherry. The two were traveling to Orlando, Florida, to play a game against the Twins when they started talking about Sandy's troubles. Sherry told Sandy that he had a simple solution.

"If you get behind the hitter, don't try to throw hard," he told Sandy. (Getting behind the hitter is falling behind in the count.) "When you force your fastball, you're always high with it. Just this once, try it my way." Sandy agreed. He'd give Sherry's approach a try. After all, it was just a spring training game, so he had very little to lose. Together, they planned to start the game with more curveballs and changeups to mix things up a bit. Then Sandy could come at the hitters with more relaxed and controlled fastballs.

At first, the experiment was looking like a disaster. Sandy was wilder than ever. He quickly slipped back into his pattern of trying to overpower every hitter. He lost patience with the other pitches and just wanted to go back to the fastball over and over.

---

66 *He had a lot of trouble finding home plate. It was ball one, ball two, and he'd shake me off, wanting to throw a fastball. And he'd throw it and it was high, and that was part of the problem. He threw a lot of fastballs up and out of the [strike] zone and guys wouldn't swing at them.* 99

—NORM SHERRY, DODGERS CATCHER

Sherry went to the mound and reminded Sandy about what they'd discussed. With his own approach failing, Sandy gave it another shot. And as soon as he relaxed and stopped trying to force every pitch, everything came together. When he wasn't concentrating on throwing the ball at full speed, his control was spot-on. And as a bonus, he discovered that he wasn't even really losing any speed on his pitches. They were going just as fast as before. But now they were going where he wanted them to go. Sandy struck out the next three hitters and went on to pitch seven innings of no-hit ball. Sherry later said that he could tell right away that something had happened. In an afternoon, Sandy Koufax had become a brand-new pitcher.

"Here's a guy who since [1955] has been trying to make it in the major leagues and always had the same problem," Sherry said. "And what, a couple of words like, 'Don't try to throw so hard,' is going to change him? It hit home, but it takes time for pitchers to find themselves. But he did it, and he became dominant."

After the game, Sandy went out with pitcher Larry Sherry—Norm's brother—to celebrate. They got back to camp after their curfew and had to face a very angry Walter Alston, who fined them one hundred dollars each. But Sandy felt like it was money well spent.

With his newfound approach, Sandy continued to work on his control. The team statistician talked to him about the importance of getting ahead in the count, showing him the statistics that proved what a difference it makes. From that point on, Sandy's goal was always to get a strike on the first pitch to every hitter.

"In the past, I'd try to throw every pitch harder than the last one," he said. "From then on I tried to throw strikes and make them hit the ball. The whole difference was control. Not just controlling the ball, but controlling myself too."

The changes were dramatic, and once the 1961 season began, Sandy and the Dodgers were reaping the rewards. He earned a regular spot in the starting rotation and roared out to a 9–2 start. Among those wins was a 2-hit, 14-strikeout shutout of the Chicago Cubs. Later came a classic pitcher's duel with Bob Gibson, which Sandy and the Dodgers won 1–0. Asked about his sudden success, Sandy answered, "If there was a magic formula, it was getting to pitch every fourth day."

Sandy's transformation was getting league-wide attention. In July he was named to the National League All-Star team. Sandy's time in the limelight was brief; he had just a ninth-inning appearance in the first of two All-Star games. (From 1959 to 1962, Major League Baseball held two All-Star games.) After that game, he struggled a bit, although not as badly as he had struggled in earlier seasons. But through it all, he continued to put up big strikeout numbers. By September, Sandy was chasing Christy Matthewson's NL record of 267 strikeouts in a season. Meanwhile, the Dodgers were chasing the Reds for the pennant.

On September 15, Sandy struck out fifteen batters in an 11–2 win over the Braves. The win pulled the Dodgers to within four and a half games of the Reds. Despite the team's hard push toward first place, they just didn't have enough to catch Cincinnati.

But that didn't stop Sandy from passing Matthewson. He finally got the record-breaking strikeout in the sixth inning of a game against the Phillies. He zoomed a fastball past Pancho Herrera for his 268th strikeout and the NL record.

Sandy's record should have been a big deal, but many fans barely noticed. Their attention was fixed on Mickey Mantle and Roger Maris of the New York Yankees. The "M&M boys" were both closing in on Babe Ruth's record of sixty home runs in a single season. Mantle fell behind in September, but Maris went on to hit sixty-one homers that year. In another year, Sandy would have received more attention. But not in 1961.

---

66 *A guy breaks a record that has stood for fifty-eight seasons, and he gets treated as if he has the German measles.* **99**

—STAN HOCHMAN, THE *PHILADELPHIA DAILY NEWS*

Still, it had been an amazing season for Sandy. After six years of failure, he was finally the pitcher the Dodgers had been imagining when they signed him to a big bonus in 1955. He was still learning, but his combination of power and newfound control was already beginning to dominate hitters. He finished the year at 18–13—just short of his goal of a twenty-win season—with an ERA of 3.52. His mark of 269 strikeouts in a season had broken a record that had stood for more than fifty years, and he had done it in just 255⅔ innings of work. Most important, he was issuing fewer walks per game than ever before. He had the confidence to put any of his pitches wherever he wanted it. At the end of the season, Sandy found himself in an unfamiliar position: he was actually looking forward to the next year.

The 1962 season was a time of change for baseball. The New York Mets entered the league as an expansion team, largely to take the place of the departed Giants and Dodgers. Meanwhile, the Dodgers left their home at the Coliseum and moved into a new ballpark, Chavez Ravine (also called Dodger Stadium). The new stadium was great for Sandy, Drysdale, and the other pitchers. With its long fences and heavy ocean air, it was one of the most pitcher-friendly parks in baseball.

Sandy's first start came against the Reds on "Chinatown Night" at the new ballpark. As part of the celebration, Sandy was carried onto the field on a rickshaw (a small Asian cart with a seat, pulled by another person). After allowing a soft hit to his first batter (on a ball that an outfielder lost in the glare of the stadium lights), Sandy was on fire. He didn't allow another hit for the next eight innings. Despite giving up three hits in the ninth, he walked off the field with a 6–2 win.

That was only the beginning. Sandy was building on his 1961 success. He dominated the opposition, pitching masterfully in game after game and establishing himself as the best pitcher in baseball.

On April 24 in Chicago, Sandy found himself chasing the single-game strikeout record he shared with Bob Feller. He started the game by striking out the side (all three hitters) in the first inning. He recorded at least one strikeout in every inning except the sixth. By the time he took the mound with a big lead in the ninth, he had fifteen strikeouts. Calmly, he notched strikeouts sixteen, seventeen, and eighteen to tie the record. Of the 144 pitches he threw that day, 96 were for strikes.

BULLPEN ANTICS

Sandy was so good in 1962 that the Dodgers relievers joked that they didn't even have to come to work on the days he pitched. They came up with all kinds of ways to entertain themselves while Sandy hurled one complete game after the next. They even invented an elaborate plan to rob a bank during a game because with Sandy on the mound, nobody would miss them!

"I lost track of how many strikeouts I had today," he told reporters. "I didn't know I'd tied the record until the game was over and everybody came off the bench to shake my hand."

After the game, some reporters and fans began calling Sandy "the human strikeout machine."

Sandy kept rolling. At one point, he pitched four straight complete games. One of the most memorable was in the Dodgers' return to New York to face the Mets. Sandy had pitched in the team's last game in New York years before, so it was only fitting that he got the start in their return to the state. The crowd was wild, standing and screaming almost the entire game. While Sandy struggled at times, the Dodgers scored thirteen runs for him, which was more than enough. Afterward, Sandy called it the most exciting game of his life.

On June 13, Sandy faced off against pitching legend Warren Spahn in Milwaukee. He pitched a great game, giving up just one run, but the real story was that Sandy won the game with his bat. His home run off forty-one-year-old Spahn gave the Dodgers a 2–1 win. An angry Spahn threw down his glove and yelled at the young lefty, who was happily skipping around the bases. Sandy was thrilled. Hitting his first career homer would have been big under any circumstance. But hitting it against a baseball legend to win the game was almost too good to be true.

Next Sandy beat Bob Gibson 1–0, just as he had in 1961. But despite his amazing run of success, not everything was perfect. Sandy was having problems with his left index finger. Blood wasn't circulating properly into the finger, leaving it cold and numb. Because Sandy didn't rely on that finger to grip his pitches, it didn't seem like a big deal.

On June 30, Sandy took his game to a new level in a home game against the Mets. From the first inning on, his stuff (pitching) was even better than usual. The struggling Mets, who would go on to lose 120 games in their first year (a modern-day record), didn't have a chance. After striking out, outfielder Richie Ashburn walked back to the Mets' dugout and said that Sandy had just thrown the fastest pitch he'd ever seen.

Sandy got out of the first inning by striking out the side on a total of nine pitches. He called it the best inning he'd ever pitched.

The rest of the game also went pretty well. Soon, the crowd was buzzing—Sandy had a no-hitter going. Solly Hemus, New York's third base coach, walked up to Sandy and reminded him of the no-hitter, hoping to make the twenty-six-year-old nervous. But it didn't work. In the ninth inning, Sandy walked the leadoff hitter but then got two quick outs on ground balls. The crowd was on its feet, roaring—one out to go. Felix Mantilla was New York's last hope. Sandy got him to ground out to end the game. Teammates and fans swarmed the field to congratulate Sandy on his first career no-hitter.

After the game, Mets manager Casey Stengel said, "You put the whommy [bad luck] on him, but when he's pitching, the whommy tends to go on vacation."

Sandy was simply dominating every time he took the mound. But after his no-hitter, his left index finger grew worse. It was a sickly shade of white, a clear sign that blood wasn't flowing properly into it.

On July 8, Sandy pitched the final game before the All-Star break. The finger had turned deep red and felt sore. Sandy couldn't put any pressure on it. Because of the pain, he could only throw his fastball. Somehow, one pitch was enough—he carried a no-hitter into the sixth inning and a one-hitter into the ninth. But by that time, he was losing feeling in his finger, and Drysdale had to come in to seal the victory.

Sandy didn't play in the All-Star game because of the finger, but he did make his next start after the break. The finger had gone from red to blue. In addition, he had a big blood blister on the tip. But Sandy kept on pitching, and pitching well. He'd thrown six shutout innings against the Mets when the blister finally popped. When the blood that came out was a pale pink rather than a healthy red, Sandy knew that it was time to do something.

At first, doctors didn't know what was wrong. Their tests showed that the finger was getting only about 15 percent of its normal blood flow. They thought that he might have a blood clot or a circulation disorder called Raynaud's phenomenon. In the end, they decided it must be a crushed artery.

Sandy Koufax attended the University of Cincinnati for one year, where he played basketball and baseball. The eighteen-year-old had a great arm, but he sometimes struggled with his control.

Sandy Koufax joined the Brooklyn Dodgers in 1955. By 1958 the team had moved to Los Angeles, and Sandy had become a star pitcher.

In game one of the 1963 World Series, Sandy faced New York Yankees ace Whitey Ford. Both men had excellent seasons, but on this day Sandy was the better pitcher, striking out fifteen batters for a 5–2 win.

Koufax and Ford met again four days later, in game four of the World Series. Sandy continued to dominate, winning the game 2–1 and giving the Dodgers the championship. His teammates mobbed him immediately after second baseman Dick Tracewski made the final out of the game.

For most of his career, Sandy relied on two pitches: the fastball and the curveball. Batters said that even when they could tell what pitch he was throwing, they still couldn't hit it.

Sandy poses with a few of his 1963 awards. That year he won the Cy Young Award for best pitcher and was named Major League Player of the Year and World Series Most Valuable Player.

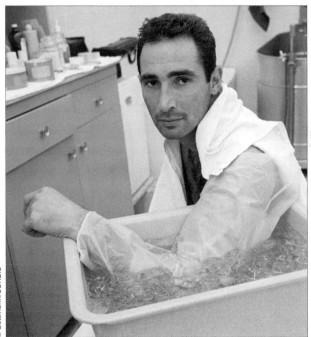

Even as he dazzled batters and base-ball fans with his powerful left arm, Sandy struggled with arthritis in his elbow. He had to soak his arm in ice water after every game to relieve the swelling.

On September 9, 1965, Sandy Koufax pitched a perfect game in Los Angeles against the Chicago Cubs. Here, Sandy faces Chris Krug in the ninth inning. Krug struck out, as did the final two Cubs batters that evening.

Sandy retired from baseball after the 1966 season. In 1972, at age thirty-six, he became the youngest person ever elected into the National Baseball Hall of Fame.

In 1999 Sandy was named to the All Century Team—the top thirty players from the past one hundred years. Sandy *(center)* stands with *(left to right)* pitchers Roger Clemens, Bob Gibson, Nolan Ryan, and Warren Spahn.

The diagnosis was grim. Doctors believed there was a very good chance that they might have to amputate Sandy's finger. For ten days, Sandy underwent experimental procedures to fix the problem. Finally, the medications did the trick, restoring blood flow to the finger. He was going to be okay. "You're very lucky," his doctor told him. "You don't know how close you came to losing the finger."

A COSTLY DECISION

While Sandy was seeing doctors about his bad finger, he realized when the problem might have started. In a game that April, Sandy had tried batting from the left side of the plate (he usually hit right-handed). Earl Francis of the Pirates threw a hard inside pitch that Sandy hit off the handle of his bat. The handle of the bat pinched into his hand and probably crushed an artery in the finger.

The injury caused Sandy to miss two months of the season. It was a devastating blow to the Dodgers, who had been in first place when he left the team. When Sandy finally returned, only eight games remained in a tight NL pennant race. The Dodgers were in a full collapse, with their once-huge lead dwindling fast to the up-and-coming Giants.

Eager to help, Sandy rushed back and took the mound on September 21. But his return was a disaster, and he didn't even survive the first inning. Clearly, he had come back too soon. He was much better in his second start, retiring his first eleven batters, but by the fifth inning, he was tiring. He didn't have his stamina back yet. The Dodgers' lead, meanwhile, continued to shrink. By season's end, they were tied for first place with the Giants. A best-of-three-game playoff would determine which team would advance to the World Series.

Sandy started game one of the playoff series. With a Willie Mays home run, the Giants jumped out to a 2–0 lead in the first inning. Sandy gave up another homer in the second and was soon pulled from the game. The Giants won the game 8–0 and went on to win the series.

Sandy and the Dodgers ended the season on a disappointing note. But it was still a remarkable year. Sandy finished at 14–7 with a league-leading ERA of 2.54. In just $184\frac{1}{3}$ innings, he struck out 216 while walking only 57. If not for the injury, he almost certainly would have won twenty games for the first time in his career and would have been the favorite to win the Cy Young Award as baseball's best pitcher. Dodger fans could only wonder what might have been if not for Sandy's injured finger.

Chapter Seven

Baseball's Best

Sandy tried not to let "what-ifs" bother him. During the off-season, he was even able to laugh at all the concern fans and reporters had about his finger. In February 1963, he joined entertainer Milton Berle in Las Vegas, Nevada, to take part in a skit that poked fun at him.

"How's the finger?" Berle asked.

"I've been to the doctor and he says it shouldn't bother me at all," Sandy replied. "But now I've got a little problem with my thumb." Sandy then brought his left hand out from behind his back, showing an oversized thumb covered in big bandages.

As good as 1962 had been, Sandy hoped 1963 would be even better. After winning three of his first five games, Sandy took the mound on May 11 to face his team's biggest rival—the Giants. The opposing pitcher that day was the ace of the Giants' staff, Juan Marichal.

At first Sandy didn't feel like he had his best stuff. But he survived the early innings untouched and only grew stronger as the game wore on. Entering the eighth inning, Sandy didn't just have a no-hitter in the works—he had a perfect game (allowing no base runners at all). But when his 3–2 fastball to Ed Bailey missed low, Bailey walked to first and the Giants had a runner on.

The bid for a perfect game was over, but with a score of 8–0, the game was well in hand for the Dodgers. All that remained was Sandy's quest for a no-hitter. With two outs in the ninth, Sandy walked the dangerous Willie McCovey on four pitches to get to Harvey Kuenn. The Giants' outfielder swung at a 0–1 pitch and grounded it weakly back to the mound. Sandy scooped it up, ran a few steps toward first base, then tossed it underhand for the final out. He'd completed his second career no-hitter. And this time, it had come against the defending NL champs, not against the worst team in baseball. Sandy jumped with his arms in the air as his teammates rushed onto the field to celebrate.

"It's too bad I walked those two guys," Sandy said after the game. "But it is still my greatest thrill."

Sandy continued his domination of the National League throughout the first half of the season. By the All-Star break, he'd compiled a 14–3 record—the same record he'd had at the halfway point of the 1962 season. This time, however, there was no finger injury to slow him down. He planned to be with his team all season to help them hold the lead they'd built in the NL standings.

SWING AND A MISS

Like many pitchers, Sandy wasn't much of a hitter. His lifetime batting average was just .097, and he struck out in 386 of his 776 at bats. But he did manage to hit two home runs during his career, one in 1962 and another in 1963.

The 1963 Dodgers may have been the best overall team Sandy played with in his career. They had three brilliant starting pitchers—Koufax, Drysdale, and Johnny Podres. And while their lineup wasn't stocked with power hitters, it was speedy and gave the pitchers the run support they needed.

Sandy continued his brilliance, winning his twentieth game by the beginning of September. He took a short leave from the team to be with his dad, who had suffered a mild heart attack, but soon returned to keep racking up the victories.

As fall approached, the Giants were fading. The red-hot Cardinals became the Dodgers' biggest threat for the pennant. During one stretch late in the season, the Cards went 19–1 and trimmed the Dodgers' lead to a single game. In mid-September, the two teams met at St. Louis's Busch Stadium for a series that could decide the pennant.

After the Dodgers won a tight first game, it was Sandy's turn to pitch. A win would give the Dodgers a three-game lead in the standings, while a loss would drop the margin back to one game. With such high stakes, Sandy Koufax was the last person St. Louis fans wanted to see on the mound.

Once again, Sandy was nearly flawless. The Dodgers took an early 1–0 lead, and Sandy did his best to protect it. The only real threat he faced came in the third inning, when a hit batsman and a throwing error put runners at second and third with one out. Infielder Julian Javier tapped a ground ball to shortstop Maury Wills, who fielded it and gunned down the runner at home plate. Sandy then got the third out, ending the rally.

❝ *There was no one better than Sandy Koufax. Some guys throw hard, but not as consistently hard as he did. And he had good stuff for nine innings. He was the best I ever saw.* ❞

—FORMER PIRATES' SECOND BASEMAN BILL MAZEROSKI

Sandy carried a no-hitter into the seventh inning. He faced fan favorite Stan Musial, who was playing his final season in the big leagues. On an 0–1 count, Musial drove the ball into left field for a hard single, ending the no-hit bid. But Sandy retired the side without any more damage, and the Dodgers scored three more runs in the top of the eighth.

Sandy gave up three more hits in the final two innings, but he didn't allow a run. He earned his eleventh shutout of the year, giving up just four hits and no walks. "I probably had the best control of my life," he said.

Those who had watched Sandy's performance were in awe. "If he pitched a no-hitter every time, I wouldn't be a bit surprised," said Drysdale.

The next day, the Dodgers won a thrilling extra-inning game to sweep the series and take a commanding four-game lead in the NL standings. The team's September collapse a year before had become a distant memory.

During his brilliant 1963 season, Sandy's fans gave him the nickname "Special K," after the cereal. In baseball the letter *K* also stands for strikeouts.

At the end of the regular season, Sandy's numbers were stunning. His record stood at 25–5, while his ERA was an amazing 1.88. He'd also broken his own NL record for strike-outs in a season, with 306. Best of all, he'd remained healthy the entire season and had led his team to the World Series. After the season, he was showered with awards. Most notably, the Baseball Writers' Association voted him as the first unanimous winner of the Cy Young Award. He also won the National League MVP Award, a rarity for a pitcher.

The Dodgers' World Series opponent was the New York Yankees, nicknamed the Bronx Bombers. The Yankees were the defending champions and baseball's true powerhouse. Although the Dodgers had won an impressive 99 games during the regular season, the Yankees had won 104. Sluggers Mickey Mantle and Roger Maris led a potent lineup, while Whitey Ford and Jim Bouton headed up a formidable pitching staff. The Yankees were so good in 1963 that some people were suggesting that they might be the best team in baseball history.

The Dodgers, however, had something to say about that. No matter what the public thought, they always believed they could beat the mighty Yankees. And they knew that if they did, it would be on the left arm of Sandy Koufax.

Baseball fans could hardly wait for game one, which pitted baseball's two best pitchers—Koufax (25–5) and Ford (24–7)—against each other. More than 69,000 people packed themselves into Yankee Stadium, and reporters were everywhere. Yet somehow, in the hours leading up to the game, Sandy remained calm. He was even telling jokes to keep his teammates loose.

Before the 1963 World Series, a New York newspaper ran a story announcing that Sandy had been adopted. A reporter found his biological father and tried to arrange for him to get together with Sandy. But Sandy had little interest in meeting the man who had abandoned him and his mother more than twenty years before. The two never met.

Ford set the tone in the top of the first inning by striking out two, but Sandy did him one better in the bottom half by striking out the side. After the Dodgers exploded for four runs in the second inning, all Sandy had to do was keep throwing strikes. He did exactly that, striking out Mantle and then Maris to begin the bottom of the second. He had five straight strikeouts, tying a World Series record. It was a fantastic start.

The Dodgers added a run in the third, and Sandy was in his groove. The Yankee hitters were amazed by how good his stuff was. After he struck out second baseman Bobby Richardson (who had struck out only 22 times in 630 at bats during the regular season) for the second time, Richardson walked past

Mantle in the dugout. The star center fielder mumbled, "I might as well not even go up there."

Taking a perfect game into the fifth, Sandy struck out batter after batter. Before long, even the Yankee fans were cheering the Brooklyn-born Dodger. Everyone was in awe of his ability. One reporter wrote, "Koufax seemed alone, a man engaged in a game of manual solitaire. Only occasionally are you aware of the other eight men on the field."

Despite giving up two runs in the eighth, Sandy was still feeling good. His third strikeout of Richardson to end the inning had run his game total to fourteen, tying him with former teammate Carl Erskine for the World Series record.

With two outs in the ninth, Sandy still needed one more strikeout to break the record. With a runner on first and a 5–2 lead, Sandy looked in to see pinch hitter Harry Bright at the plate. Sandy remembered Bright from when he'd played for the Pirates and knew exactly how to pitch him. He threw nothing but fastballs. On a 2–2 count, Sandy fired in one last heater. Bright swung and missed. Sandy had the record! More important, the Dodgers had the game one win and had proved that they were good enough to play with the heavily favored Yankees.

After the game, Yankee catcher Yogi Berra uttered what may be the most famous words ever said about Sandy: "I can see how he won twenty-five games. What I don't understand is how he lost five." Richardson agreed, saying, "I've never seen anything like him."

Game two didn't get any better for the Yankees. Johnny Podres continued what Sandy had started, shutting down the Yankee lineup in a 4–1 Dodger win. Suddenly, the underdog Dodgers were up 2–0 in the series. Better still, they were headed back to the familiar surroundings of Chavez Ravine with a chance to win the series in front of their own fans.

The Dodger bats quieted in game three, scoring only a single run. But Drysdale threw a three-hit shutout of the Yankees, earning a 1–0 victory in what may have been the best game of his career. The Dodgers' series lead was 3–0, with Koufax and Ford set to face off again in game four.

❝ *You don't try for big innings against Sandy Koufax because you're not going to get them.* ❞

—Giants manager Alvin Dark

The pitching matchup was everything fans had hoped for this time around. Both of the left-handers were on fire, although each made one big mistake in the middle innings. (Sandy gave up a home run to Mantle, while Ford allowed one to Frank Howard.) Ford was especially brilliant, allowing only two hits all day, both by Howard. He later called it one of the best games he ever pitched.

But despite his efforts, Ford also had some bad luck. In the seventh inning, a rare three-base error on first baseman Joe Pepitone led to a second Dodger run. With Sandy on the mound and only two innings to go, a one-run lead was huge.

The top of the ninth was dangerous for Sandy, with the heart of the Yankee lineup scheduled to hit (although Maris missed the game with an injury). Richardson led off with a single. After Sandy struck out Tom Tresh, it was Mantle's turn again. The fans in the stands didn't know whether to scream or hold their breath.

Sandy got strikes one and two on fastballs. It was his best pitch, and Mantle knew it. So when Sandy threw a curveball on the next pitch, Mantle was completely surprised. The curve froze the Yankee slugger, who could only watch as it sailed through the strike zone. The umpire called, "Strike three," and the stadium went wild. One out to go.

Elston Howard was next. When Howard hit a ground ball to the shortstop, Sandy began to leap in celebration. But second baseman Dick Tracewski dropped the throw, and the Yankees were still alive, now with runners at first and second.

Sandy, who had thought the game was over, had to calm himself and get one more out. Outfielder Hector Lopez swung at Sandy's first pitch, hitting another ground ball to the short-stop. This time, Tracewski caught the throw for the force out. The Dodgers were the World Series champions, and Sandy could finally have his celebration.

"I had two great thrills that inning," Sandy said. "One when I *thought* it was over. Two when I *knew* it was over."

By leading the league in wins, strikeouts, and ERA in 1963, Sandy won what some call pitching's Triple Crown.

It was a remarkable accomplishment for Sandy and the Dodgers. They'd swept the powerful Bronx Bombers. Even more impressive, the Yankees had never even held a lead in the series. In the four games, the Yankee lineup had scored a dismal four runs against the Dodger pitching. For his two complete game wins, Sandy was named the World Series MVP. It was the perfect way to end one of the best seasons any pitcher has ever had.

Sandy was an instant celebrity after his heroics in the 1963 World Series. He was finally being paid like a star player, even though he didn't think his new salary of $70,000 per year was enough. He used some of his money to buy a house for himself.

He also bought a house in California for his parents so he could be with them more often.

Meanwhile, he had a new problem to deal with—the demands of a hungry media. Everyone wanted a piece of Sandy Koufax. A naturally private man, all the attention was a burden on him. When he wasn't as available as some of the reporters might have liked, he earned a reputation as a recluse. The truth was that Sandy was just embarrassed by all of the attention.

Chapter Eight

Staying on Top

After a season like Sandy and the Dodgers had enjoyed in 1963, expectations were understandably high for 1964. But as early as spring training, Sandy had a notion that trouble might lie ahead. With his over-the-top delivery and sheer power, a sore arm was an expected sacrifice. But as the new season got under way, the soreness in Sandy's left arm was worse than usual. The arm always hurt after a game, and his ritual of soaking it in ice water after games had long since been established. But for the first time, the pain was affecting his pitch selection. Early in the season, he wasn't throwing his best pitch—the fastball—nearly as often as he usually did.

Still, Sandy started things off right with a 4–0 shutout of the Cardinals to open the season. The arm hurt, but he was able to pitch through the pain. That wasn't true in his third start of the year, when he felt something wrong with his arm and had to come out after pitching just one inning. The pain was just too much. After receiving several shots of a drug called cortisone, Sandy had to sit out a couple of weeks. He struggled when he came back, dropping to 4–4 by the end of May.

One day in the locker room, Sandy was looking at an old magazine article about his no-hitter against the Giants. He noticed something in the photographs of that game—the placement of his feet during his delivery had changed from 1963 to 1964. It was a tiny difference, but even small changes in a pitcher's delivery can have a big effect. Sandy showed the photographs to the team's pitching coach, and together they worked to correct the problem.

A few days later, Sandy made his next start. Unluckily for his opponents, the Phillies, the minor adjustment solved the problem and Sandy was back to his old, dominating self. He was nearly perfect early, allowing just a fourth-inning walk on a close 3–2 pitch to Richie Allen.

As the innings crawled by, Sandy remained unhittable. He had the pop back in his fastball, and his curves were breaking hard. When he struck out pinch hitter Bobby Wine on a fastball to end the ninth, he had done it again—it was his third career no-hitter. He had become only the fourth pitcher in major league history to throw three in a career and just the second to do it in the modern era (post-1900). Nobody had ever thrown a no-hitter in three consecutive years. To say his small adjustment worked would be an understatement.

"This was the best of them, the best of them all," Sandy told reporters when asked to compare his three no-hitters.

> ❝ *I go up and I know none of these [fans] are rooting for me. Let's face it, there were not a lot of people outside my family rooting for me. Guys on the on-deck circle were saying, . . . 'I hope he makes an out so I don't have to hit.'* ❞
>
> —BOBBY WINE ON MAKING THE LAST OUT
> IN SANDY'S THIRD CAREER NO-HITTER

Sandy was finally living up to his high personal expectations. The no-hitter sparked a stretch in which he won ten of his next eleven games. But despite his efforts, the team was floundering. Podres was hurt, leaving Sandy and Drysdale as the only two reliable starters. And the offense was struggling badly. The team was stuck near the bottom of the standings, and it was clear that they wouldn't be returning to the World Series in October.

Things got even worse in August. In a game against the Braves, Sandy had gotten a hit and stood on second base. As Milwaukee pitcher Tony Cloninger prepared to throw his next pitch, Sandy stepped out to a small lead off the base. Cloninger spun and fired the ball to the base in an attempt to pick him off. Sandy dove back to the bag. As he touched the base, the second baseman swept a hard tag against his left arm, stinging his elbow.

Despite the pain, Sandy stayed in the game and came around to score. The Dodgers got a 5–4 win, but it had come at a steep price. Sandy's arm was swollen and very painful.

Somehow, he managed to start (and win) his next two games, pushing his record to 19–5. He'd won fifteen of his last sixteen contests, and his ERA of 1.74 was the best in the league and the best of his career. But Sandy never got the chance to win his twentieth. The morning after his final start, his arm was in so much pain and so swollen that he couldn't even straighten it.

Soon after, Sandy learned that his season was over. The tag had done serious damage to an arm that had already suffered so much abuse. Worse still, he had a condition called arthritis that made his joints stiff and sore. He'd had the condition for years, but the tag had made it much worse.

"I could see it blow up," Sandy said, describing how his elbow swelled when he tried to move it. "It sounded as if I were squeezing a soggy sponge."

Sandy and his doctors knew that his arthritis had no cure. It wasn't a condition that would simply go away. In fact, the opposite was true. As long as Sandy continued to abuse his arm by pitching, the arthritis could only grow worse. All that they could hope to do was manage the pain and swelling.

During his extended off-season, Sandy focused on resting the arm. For more than four months, he didn't even pick up a baseball. His arm needed, he said, the "healing touch of winter."

Early in spring training of 1965, all of the signs about the health of Sandy's arm were good. The terrible pain was gone, and he had his full range of motion back. Things were going so well that he threw a complete spring training game at the end of March—a rarity at that time of the year even for a healthy pitcher.

The next morning, Sandy asked his roommate Dick Tracewski to look at the arm. "The elbow was black," Tracewski said. "And it was swollen. There was muscles that were pulled and there was hemorrhaging. From the elbow to the armpit, it looked like a bruise. . . . It was an angry arm, an angry elbow."

Sandy returned to his doctor. The prognosis was grim—it seemed that Sandy's arm simply wouldn't hold up. He might not be able to fill a regular spot in the starting rotation. They started talking about pitching him less often—every five days or even once a week. But Sandy had another idea. If the point of starting him less often was to reduce wear and tear on his arm, he would simply stop throwing between starts. The only time he'd throw a baseball would be during a game. Everyone agreed—it was worth a shot.

Sandy's regimen to keep his arm going quickly became famous. It was a mixture of fire and ice. The fire came in the form of Capsolin, a salve (cream) made from the extract of hot peppers. Sandy applied the burning salve to the arm regularly. It stung and smelled terrible, but it also helped to manage the pain in his joints. The ice came in after a game. Trainers fitted Sandy with a rubber sleeve to wear while he held his arm in a bucket of frigid ice water. The sleeve protected his skin while the numbing cold managed his swelling. Meanwhile, he took a variety of drugs to control both the pain and the swelling. One writer called Sandy "America's favorite medical project." It wasn't an easy way to make a living, but the regimen allowed the game's most dominating pitcher to do what he did best.

Finally, the 1965 season began. Sandy didn't have his best stuff in his first appearance against the Phillies. But he still managed to earn a 6–2 win. The victory was nice, but what Dodger players, coaches, and fans really cared about was the next morning. How would Sandy's arm respond?

The news was good. The elbow was a bit swollen, but not badly. The regimen had worked. Sandy would be able to make his normal starts.

Once he was back in the routine of pitching regularly, Sandy was back to his old self. He won five of his first seven decisions, including a complete-game, eleven-inning marathon against Houston. From there, he kept on rolling. On August 10, he defeated the Mets 4–3 to notch his twentieth win of the season. Meanwhile, the Dodgers were in first place in a very tight pennant race with the Braves and the Giants.

But over the next month, things began to go downhill. The Dodger offense dried up. Sandy and the other pitchers were a bit off. The Dodgers' lead in the NL standings dwindled.

The tension of the tight race boiled over on August 22 before a crowd of 42,807 at San Francisco's Candlestick Park. The Giants and Dodgers were already fierce rivals, and the stakes were high. In the final game of the heated series, each team sent its ace to the mound—Koufax versus Marichal.

Everything was going smoothly until Los Angeles took a 2–1 lead. Marichal responded by pitching inside to several Dodger hitters. It was a tactic he used to intimidate the hitters, and one the Dodgers didn't like.

When Marichal's turn to bat came, catcher John Roseboro wanted Sandy to brush him back with an inside fastball. It would be a message telling Marichal to stop throwing inside to the Dodger hitters. But Sandy didn't want to do it—a pitcher who brushes back the other team's pitcher stands to receive the same treatment during his next plate appearance.

Roseboro decided to send the message on his own. After Sandy's first pitch to Marichal, Roseboro intentionally threw the ball back to the mound so that it whizzed right past Marichal's head. The Giants pitcher said the ball nicked his ear (film of the event is inconclusive) and went wild with anger. He lifted his bat and slammed it down on Roseboro's head. The blow opened a huge, bloody gash, and both benches emptied. Sandy rushed in from the mound to protect his teammate and friend from further injury.

Marichal's explosion and the brawl that followed remain among the darkest images in baseball history. After peace was finally restored (with help from the police) and Marichal was ejected, the game resumed. Sandy, shaken by what had happened, had to return to the mound. He wasn't able to get the incident out of his mind, though, and went on to give up a three-run homer to Willie Mays. The home run gave the Giants a 4–3 win and reduced the Dodgers' lead in the standings to half a game.

"Sandy was shook up," Mays said. "After what happened, Sandy didn't have his real good stuff."

The loss was just another part of the Dodgers' downward spiral. Even Sandy couldn't get a win. He lost five decisions in a row at one point. The Dodgers slipped four and a half games out of first place with just a few weeks to go. When Sandy faced the Cubs on September 9, the outlook was bleak for the Dodger faithful.

In the early innings of the game, both starting pitchers were brilliant. Through four innings, both Sandy and the Cubs'

Bob Hendley had no-hitters. In the fifth, the Dodgers scored a run without the benefit of a hit to take a 1–0 lead.

By the seventh, Hendley was working on a one-hitter while Sandy had yet to allow a base runner. After striking out the side in the eighth, Sandy was just three outs away from one of the rarest of baseball achievements: a perfect game.

Chris Krug and Joey Amalfitano each went down swinging to start the ninth. As Amalfitano walked back to the dugout, the next hitter, Harvey Kuenn, told him, "Wait here, Joe. I'll be right back."

Sure enough, he was. Sandy fell behind in the count early, 2–1. From the radio booth, Vin Scully wondered if Sandy was feeling the pressure. "You can't blame a man for pushing just a little bit now," he said.

After stepping off the mound to relax himself, Sandy fired two straight strikes past the swinging Kuenn. An excited Scully said, "Swung on and missed, a perfect game!"

Twice a Victim

Harvey Kuenn made the final out in two of Sandy's no-hitters—first as a Giant in 1963, then as a Cub in 1965. When someone asked him what the difference between the two games was, Kuenn answered, "About two years."

It was Sandy's sixth strikeout in a row, and it completed one of the most remarkable pitching duels in history. Hendley's fantastic one-hitter was all but forgotten in the shadow of Sandy's perfect game.

"I got stronger as I went along," Sandy said. "In the last three innings, I had my best fastball in a long, long time."

Shortly after the big win, the Dodgers caught fire, winning thirteen games in a row. They launched back into first place, thanks in big part to the left arm of Sandy Koufax, who struck out a record 382 batters that season. His record of 26–8 and ERA of 2.04 led the league, and he cruised to another Cy Young Award. But more important, the Dodgers ended the season atop the NL standings. They'd earned themselves a trip to Minnesota for the World Series.

A problem soon became apparent, however. Sandy was the obvious choice to start game one, but the game fell on the same day as Yom Kippur, the holiest of Jewish holidays. Faithful Jews don't work on Yom Kippur, and Sandy had always set the day aside for prayer. His decision was an easy one—he wouldn't pitch. He had to put his faith ahead of his team.

Sandy was disappointed that he'd have to let his teammates down, but he also kept up his sense of humor. He said that he prayed for rain that day so the ballgame would be postponed. No rain came, though, so Drysdale started in Sandy's place.

The Twins hit Drysdale hard, knocking him from the game in the second inning. When Alston came out to remove Drysdale from the game, the big right-hander joked, "I bet right now you wish I was Jewish too."

The Twins won game one easily, then won again the next day when Sandy had uncharacteristic control problems. "I was high with the fastball when I wanted it low," Sandy said. "And when I was trying to get it up, it was down."

Things looked bad for the Dodgers. But on returning to Los Angeles, they took games three and four to tie the series. Game five would belong to Sandy. He wasn't about to let down his teammates again. The series would head back to Minnesota after the game. If the Dodgers lost, they'd need to win two in a row in Met Stadium—a very difficult task.

This time, Sandy had his good stuff and outdueled Kaat. He allowed only four hits—all singles—as the Dodgers cruised to a 7–0 win. After being down 0–2, they had stormed back to take the series lead.

❝ *We were beaten by a great pitcher. [Koufax is] the best I've ever seen.*❞

—TWINS MANAGER SAM MELE

After the game, Sandy told a reporter that he felt a hundred years old. The long season was taking its toll. But when the Twins won game six to force a final, deciding game, Sandy was there for his team.

Despite arthritis and exhaustion and despite having pitched only three days earlier, Sandy had one game left in him. And it was a gem. His second shutout of the series finished off the Twins. The Dodgers were the champions again. Asked how old he felt now, the World Series MVP joked, "A hundred and one."

Chapter | Nine

An Early End

andy knew that his arm wasn't getting any better. He would be just thirty years old by the time the 1966 season started, but he knew that he didn't have much time left. During the off-season, he decided that he was long overdue for a big raise. At the time, players had very little negotiating power. When a player signed a contract with a team, he was bound to the team for his entire career unless the team decided to trade him. Since the teams basically owned the players, they could pay whatever they pleased.

Sandy talked with Drysdale, who also felt that he deserved a raise. From 1963 to 1965, the two pitchers won a combined 130 games for the Dodgers. Together, the two pitchers hatched a plan. They would negotiate together. Neither man would sign until both got what they wanted. Maybe together they'd have the power that neither of them had alone.

They brought their contract demands to Bavasi. They each wanted a three-year, $500,000 contract—a total of $1 million between them. Bavasi laughed at their offer and wished them luck.

Sandy began to make preparations for a possible holdout. He agreed to write his autobiography, with the help of author Ed Linn. He and Drysdale also agreed to star together in a movie called *Warning Shot* (though they would only make the movie if they didn't receive contracts). Together, the two deals meant that Sandy could afford to hold out. He wouldn't have to accept a low offer just to get a paycheck.

 Sandy's career record in 1–0 games was 11–3.

By February 1966, the two pitchers had dropped their demands to $450,000 each. But the Dodgers wouldn't budge. Spring training opened without the two stars. Dodger fans grew more and more nervous with each passing day. The story dominated the sports headlines. Surprisingly, many of their fellow players criticized the holdout. But Sandy and Drysdale believed that what they were doing could be good for all players in the long run. It was about time that somebody stood up to the owners.

Finally, on March 30, the holdout ended. Bavasi offered Sandy a one-year deal worth $125,000, while Drysdale got $110,000. Eager to get back to the game, they agreed. It wasn't all they'd been hoping for, but each man got a much bigger raise than he would have negotiating on his own.

To the great relief of Dodger players and fans, the pitchers finally joined the team in spring training—more than a month late. Missing time didn't seem to bother Sandy. Meanwhile, Drysdale would struggle through one of the worst seasons of his career.

 In 1966 Sandy set an NL record by pitching 323 innings without hitting a batter.

Even though Sandy was pitching great, all was not well. He was beginning to lose feeling in the fingers on his left hand. He would drop things and had a hard time working with small objects like buttons. The damage he was doing to his arm was becoming more and more real. He returned to his doctor. This time the doctor's advice was simple and clear. Sandy could retire or risk losing the use of the arm.

It was tough news for Sandy, still just thirty years old, to hear. After all the effort to get a new contract, he didn't feel like he could stop playing then and there. He wanted to finish the year. He didn't tell anyone his long-term plans, but he already knew that the 1966 season would be his last.

Sandy didn't waste a moment. By mid-July, he was already 16–4. Once again, the Dodger offense was having trouble scoring runs, but with the game's best pitcher on the mound, it hardly mattered.

Although Sandy hadn't told anyone about his future plans, the growing severity of his condition was no secret. Those who watched him were amazed not just by his ability but by his determination and willingness to pitch through the obvious pain.

"Don't tell me about arthritis," said Pittsburgh's Roberto Clemente after facing Sandy. "How can his arm hurt if he throws that hard?"

Somehow, despite a sputtering offense and Drysdale's struggles, the Dodgers remained in the heat of the pennant race. By the last game of the season, Sandy's record stood at 26–9. If he could win the team's final game in Philadelphia, the Dodgers would clinch the NL pennant and return to the World Series.

Sandy was exhausted when he took the mound on October 2. Just three days before, he'd beaten the Cardinals in a 2–1 pitchers' duel. Now, after a long season and on just two days of rest, his tired left arm carried the hopes of Dodger fans everywhere. His offense came through for him early, scoring six runs and lifting much of the pressure. But in the fifth inning, Sandy felt a sharp pain in his back. He managed to finish the inning, then rushed back to the clubhouse for treatment. A disk in his spine had slipped out of place. The trainers popped him back into shape and sent him back out the next inning.

By the ninth, the score remained 6–0. But then Sandy started to get into trouble. Three runs scored and another runner stood on base, and Sandy still hadn't gotten anyone out. Suddenly, the pressure was back on. Sandy couldn't afford to slip up now. He took a deep breath and went after his next three hitters, retiring them on two strikeouts and a groundout to seal the win and the pennant. The Dodgers were headed back to the World Series, and Sandy was the hero once again. The win was his twenty-ninth of the season—a career high. It was also the last win he would ever get.

In Sandy's career, he struck out a total of 2,396 batters in 2,324⅓ innings pitched, making him one of only a handful of pitchers in baseball history to average more than one strikeout per inning.

The Dodgers' World Series opponent was the 97–63 Baltimore Orioles. Because Sandy had pitched the final game of the season, Drysdale started game one. The power-hitting Orioles got to him right away, scoring three runs in the first inning. The Dodgers never recovered and lost the opener 5–2.

Sandy faced off against youngster Jim Palmer in game two. Both pitchers cruised through four scoreless innings, but those who knew Sandy could see that he was suffering. His fastball just didn't have its normal zip.

In the fifth, Sandy found himself in a small jam with a runner at second base. He got outfielder Paul Blair to lift a high fly ball into center field. But Willie Davis lost the ball in the sun, and it dropped in for an error.

Sandy got the next batter to hit another fly ball to center field. But again, Davis lost it in the sun and let it fall. The rattled Davis then made a bad throw to third base for his third error of the inning—a World Series record. By the time the nightmare fifth inning was over, Baltimore had scored three runs.

Back in the dugout, Sandy headed straight for the upset Davis. One teammate tried to stop the lefty, fearing that he was about to blow up at the struggling outfielder. But Sandy didn't do that. Instead, he sat down and put his arm around Davis. "Forget it," he said.

Davis was badly shaken, though, and made another fielding blunder in the sixth, leading to another Baltimore run. Sandy finished out the sixth inning and walked off the mound in a 4–0 game. In the bottom of the sixth, Alston put in a pinch hitter for him. The Los Angeles crowd didn't know it, but they had just seen the last pitch of Sandy Koufax's brilliant career. Baltimore won the game, then took games three and four in Baltimore to complete the World Series sweep.

About a month later, Sandy called a press conference in Beverly Hills, California. Wearing a suit and tie, he stood before dozens of reporters. Flashbulbs winked in his face as he made the announcement that no Dodger fan wanted to hear—his baseball career was over.

The Dodgers desperately tried to talk Sandy out of retiring, even offering him $150,000 to return for 1967.

"I've got a lot of years to live after baseball," he explained. "I would like to live them with the complete use of my body. I have taken too many pills and too many shots. . . . I don't regret one minute of the last twelve years, but I think I would regret one year that was too many."

Sandy's final season may have been his finest. To go along with his 27–9 record, he had a career-low ERA of 1.73. He struck out 317 batters while walking only 77. He'd left baseball at the height of his dominance—at age thirty, many players are just entering their prime. Fans can only imagine what Sandy might have accomplished with a healthy left arm.

❝ *If there was a man who did not have the use of his arms and you told him it would cost a lot of money if he could buy back that use, he'd give every dime he had, I believe. That's my feeling, and in a sense, maybe this is what I'm doing.* **❞**

—SANDY KOUFAX, WHEN ASKED IF HE WOULD MISS THE
INCOME HE EARNED FROM BASEBALL

It was time to move on, though. New worlds were opening up to Sandy. In December, NBC Sports offered him a job. He agreed to serve as an analyst for the network's *Game of the Week*. It was a surprising choice to many. Sandy was a private person who often resented the demands of the media. But the money was good, and the job allowed him to keep working with the game he loved.

Sandy, who had always been calm and cool on the mound, quickly discovered that broadcasting presented a new set of challenges. In his first game as a broadcaster, he had to interview Drysdale before a Dodgers-Cardinals game. Sandy was visibly nervous, and for a few moments, he completely forgot what he was supposed to say. He got through the interview but later admitted that he was more nervous than he'd been in years.

In 1969 Sandy married Anne Widmark, the daughter of actor Richard Widmark. The couple moved to Maine, although Sandy continued to work for NBC during the season.

In 1972, at age thirty-six, Sandy became the youngest person ever elected into baseball's Hall of Fame. It was his first year of eligibility; players must wait five years after retirement before they appear on the Hall of Fame ballot. Despite having spent just twelve years in the game—and only six years at his peak—Sandy received a record 344 votes from the Baseball Writers' Association of America. "This is the biggest honor I've ever been given, not just in baseball, but in my life," he said in his induction speech.

Don Drysdale retired in 1969 because of damage to his right shoulder. He was elected to the Hall of Fame in 1984.

After the 1972 season, Sandy left NBC Sports. He was tired of the travel and wanted to enjoy a quiet life with Anne in Maine. He enjoyed cooking, golfing, and spending time with friends and family. But the marriage didn't last. After the couple divorced,

Sandy was on his own again. He spent his time doing whatever interested him—golfing, fishing, even learning to fly a plane.

"Whatever [Sandy] does, he masters it," said friend and former teammate Don Sutton. "When he gets tired of it, then he goes on and finds something else to challenge him."

Epilogue

Sandy's Legacy

In 1979 Sandy returned to the Dodgers as a minor league pitching coach. There he helped to develop some of the organization's best young arms—pitchers like Orel Hershiser, who would carry on the Dodgers' tradition of excellence. After being away for thirteen years, Sandy was happy to share his knowledge and experience with young players.

He spent more than a decade with the Dodgers before he resigned in 1990. Sandy said that he felt he was no longer useful to the team, though many people blamed a strained relationship with Dodger manager Tommy Lasorda (the same man the Dodgers had to send down to make room on the roster for Sandy in 1955). He remains involved with the Dodgers, however, and baseball is still one of his many passions.

Sandy makes few public appearances, preferring to live a quiet, private life. One of his rare appearances came during the

1999 World Series in Atlanta, Georgia, when baseball honored its All-Century Team.

He remarried briefly in the 1990s, but the marriage didn't last. Sandy returned to a single life of golfing, fishing, and enjoying time with friends and family. He lives in Vero Beach, Florida, a few miles from "Dodgertown," where the Dodgers hold spring training.

"He's not a man who wants to live in the past, certainly not his past," said Koufax biographer Jane Leavy when asked about Sandy's legendary privacy. "I think he realizes that when you do that as an athlete, which so many of them do, that . . . it's a form of cannibalizing yourself. And in order to not do that, he prefers not to indulge in personal public retrospection."

Sandy may not like to live in the past, but his fans can't help but think back to his remarkable and unique career. Sandy's career doesn't even compare well to the career of any other Hall of Famer. Three hundred wins is a benchmark for most Hall of Fame starting pitchers, yet Sandy notched only 165 in his twelve years. He spent half his career as a wildly inconsistent and underused hurler and the other half as the most dominating pitcher in baseball, with no real transition between the two. He retired at an age when most players are in the middle of their peak production. It's a career unlike any other the game has ever seen.

Fans marvel at what Sandy accomplished in such a short time but are always left wondering what might have been. What if Sandy hadn't been held back by baseball's "bonus baby rule"? What if his arm hadn't given out on him? The numbers a healthy Sandy Koufax might have tallied are almost unthinkable. Still, his years of brilliance—especially 1963 through 1966—are unmatched in baseball history, and those who saw him pitch are grateful for the years he gave us.

PERSONAL STATISTICS

Name:

Sanford Koufax

Nicknames:

Special K, the human strikeout machine

Born:

December 30, 1935

Height:

6' 2"

Weight:

210 lbs.

Residence:

Vero Beach, Florida

Threw:

Left

Batted:

Right

PITCHING STATISTICS

Year	Team	W	L	PCT	ERA	G	GS	CG	IP	H	BB	SO	SHO
1955	BRO	2	2	.500	3.02	12	5	2	41⅔	33	28	30	2
1956	BRO	2	4	.333	4.91	16	10	0	58⅔	66	29	30	0
1957	BRO	5	4	.556	3.88	34	13	2	104⅓	83	51	122	0
1958	LAD	11	11	.500	4.48	40	26	5	158⅔	132	105	131	0
1959	LAD	8	6	.571	4.05	35	23	6	153⅓	136	92	173	1
1960	LAD	8	13	.381	3.91	37	26	7	175	133	100	197	2
1961	LAD	18	13	.581	3.52	42	35	15	255⅔	212	96	269	2
1962	LAD	14	7	.667	2.54	28	26	11	184⅓	134	57	216	2
1963	LAD	25	5	.833	1.88	40	40	20	311	214	58	306	11
1964	LAD	19	5	.792	1.74	29	28	15	223	154	53	223	7
1965	LAD	26	8	.765	2.04	43	41	27	335⅔	216	71	382	8
1966	LAD	27	9	.750	1.73	41	41	27	323	241	77	317	5
	Totals	165	87	.655	2.76	397	314	137	2,324⅓	1,754	817	2,396	40
World Series (4 years)													
		4	3	.571	0.95	8	7	4	57	36	11	61	2

Key: W: wins; L: losses; PCT: percentage; ERA: earned run average; G: games; GS: games started; CG: complete games; IP: innings pitched; H: hits; BB: bases on balls (walks); SO: strikeouts; SHO: shutouts

BATTING STATISTICS

Year	Team	Avg	G	AB	Runs	Hits	2B	3B	HR	RBI	SB
1955	BRO	.000	12	12	0	0	0	0	0	0	0
1956	BRO	.118	16	17	0	2	0	0	0	0	0
1957	BRO	.000	34	26	1	0	0	0	0	0	0
1958	LAD	.122	40	49	2	6	1	0	0	1	0
1959	LAD	.111	35	54	3	6	3	0	0	0	0
1960	LAD	.123	37	57	1	7	0	0	0	1	0
1961	LAD	.065	42	77	3	5	0	0	0	2	0
1962	LAD	.087	28	69	1	6	0	0	1	4	0
1963	LAD	.064	40	110	3	7	0	0	1	7	0
1964	LAD	.095	29	74	3	7	0	0	0	1	0
1965	LAD	.177	43	113	4	20	2	0	0	7	0
1966	LAD	.076	41	118	5	9	3	0	0	5	0
	Totals	.097	397	776	26	75	9	0	2	28	0

Key: **Avg**: batting average; **G**: games; **AB**: at bats; **2B**: doubles; **3B**: triples; **HR**: home runs; **RBI**: runs batted in; **SB**: stolen bases

SOURCES

2 Jane Leavy, *Sandy Koufax: A Lefty's Legacy* (New York: HarperCollins, 2002), 188.

2 Edward Gruver, *Koufax* (Dallas, TX: Taylor Pub. Co., 2000), 32.

3 Ibid., 107.

7 Ibid., 64.

8 Ibid., 67.

8 Leavy, *Sandy Koufax*, 33.

9 Ibid., 35.

10 Ibid., 40.

12 Ibid., 47.

14 Gruver, *Koufax*, 70.

15 Ibid.

15 Leavy, *Sandy Koufax*, 49–50.

18 Ibid., 54.

18 John F. Grabowski, *Sandy Koufax* (New York: Chelsea House, 1992), 17.

18 "Sanford 'Sandy' Koufax," *Jewish Sports Hall of Fame*, n.d., http://jewishsportshalloffame.com/Hebrew/JSHF/Sandy_Koufax.htm (March 24, 2006).

22 Leavy, *Sandy Koufax*, 66.

22 Ibid., 70.

24 Gruver, *Koufax*, 94.

28 Ibid., 104.

29 Leavy, *Sandy Koufax*, 75.

31–32 Grabowski, *Sandy Koufax*, 26.

33 Leavy, *Sandy Koufax*, 86.

34 Gruver, *Koufax*, 119.

36 Ibid., 120.

37 Leavy, *Sandy Koufax*, 95.

38 Ibid., 88.

41 Ibid., 93.

42 Grabowski, *Sandy Koufax*, 30.

42 Ibid.

42 Gruver, *Koufax*, 122.

45 Leavy, *Sandy Koufax*, 92.

47 Gruver, *Koufax*, 123.

48 Leavy, *Sandy Koufax*, 95.

49 Grabowski, *Sandy Koufax*, 10.

50 Gruver, *Koufax*, 126.

51 Ibid., 127.

51–52 Schwartz, Larry, "Koufax's dominance was short but sweet," *ESPN.com*, n.d., http://espn.go.com/classic/biography/s/Koufax_Sandy.html (March 24, 2006).

52 Gruver, *Koufax*, 132.

53 Leavy, *Sandy Koufax*, 116.

55 Gruver, *Koufax*, 137.

57 Leavy, *Sandy Koufax*, 119.

59 Gruver, *Koufax*, 144.

61 Leavy, *Sandy Koufax*, 121.

62 Grabowski, *Sandy Koufax*, 40.

64 Gruver, *Koufax*, 226.

65 Ibid., 160.

65 Leavy, *Sandy Koufax*, 125.

68 Gruver, *Koufax*, 164.

68 Leavy, *Sandy Koufax*, 136.

68–69 Eric Enders, *100 Years of the World Series* (New York: Barnes & Noble Books, 2003), 159.

69 Gruver, *Koufax*, 167.

69 Ibid., 146.

71 Leavy, *Sandy Koufax*, 142.

75 Gruver, *Koufax*, 177.

75 Leavy, *Sandy Koufax*, 153.

76 Grabowski, *Sandy Koufax*, 46.

77 Gruver, *Koufax*, 180.

77 Leavy, *Sandy Koufax*, 157–158.

78 Gruver, *Koufax*, 183.

80 Ibid., 186.

81 Grabowski, *Sandy Koufax*, 48.

81 Scully, Vin, "29,000 people and a million butterflies," *Salon.com*, October 12, 1999, http://www.salon.com/people/feature/1999/10/12/scully_koufax/ (March 24, 2006).

81 Ibid.

81 Leavy, *Sandy Koufax*, 219.

82 Gruver, *Koufax*, 187.

83 Merron, Jeff, "Green, Koufax and Greenberg—same dilemma, different decisions," *ESPN.com*, September 26, 2001, http://espn.go.com/classic/s/merron_on_green.html (March 24, 2006).

83 Enders, *100 Years of the World Series*, 163.
84 Ibid., 165.
84 Gruver, *Koufax*, 195.
88 Ibid., 203.
90 Ibid., 207.
91 Ibid., 211–212.
92 Ibid., 212.
93 Ibid., 224.
94 Leavy, *Sandy Koufax*, 255.
96 "Conversation: Lefty's Legacy," *Online NewsHour*, October 21, 2002, http:// www.pbs.org/newshour/ conversation/july-dec02/leavy _10-21.html (March 24, 2006).

BIBLIOGRAPHY

Enders, Eric. *100 Years of the World Series.* New York: Barnes & Noble Books, 2003.

Gammons, Peter. *The 2005 ESPN Baseball Encyclopedia.* New York: Sterling Publishing, 2005.

Grabowski, John F. *Sandy Koufax.* New York: Chelsea House, 1992.

Gruver, Edward. *Koufax.* Dallas, TX: Taylor Pub. Co., 2000.

Koufax, Sandy, with Ed Linn. *Koufax.* New York: Viking Press, 1966.

Leavy, Jane. *Sandy Koufax: A Lefty's Legacy.* New York: HarperCollins, 2002.

Sanford, William R. and Carl R. Green. *Sandy Koufax.* New York: Crestwood House, 1993.

WEBSITES

Baseball Almanac: Sandy Koufax

http://www.baseball-almanac.com/players/player.php?p=koufasa01

Sandy's entry at Baseball-almanac.com includes detailed statistics, biographical information, and fast facts.

Los Angeles Dodgers: The Official Site

http://www.dodgers.com

The official site of the Los Angeles Dodgers includes team updates, scores, feature articles, and a historical timeline.

MLB.com

http://mlb.com

The official site of Major League Baseball has scores, news updates, video highlights, and more.

National Baseball Hall of Fame: Sandy Koufax

http://www.baseballhalloffame.org/hofers_and_honorees/hofer_bios/koufax_sandy.htm

Sandy's page at the Hall of Fame includes basic biographical information and an image of his Hall of Fame plaque.

INDEX

105